UNFIT FOR COMMAND

UNFIT FOR COMMAND

Swift Boat Veterans Speak Out
Against John Kerry

JOHN E. O'NEILL
AND JEROME R. CORSI, PH.D.

Since 1947
REGNERY
PUBLISHING, INC.
An Eagle Publishing Company • Washington, DC

Copyright © 2004 by John E. O'Neill and Jerome L. Corsi

All rights reserved. No part of this publication may be reproduced or transmitted in any form or by any means electronic or mechanical, including photocopy, recording, or any information storage and retrieval system now known or to be invented, without permission in writing from the publisher, except by a reviewer who wishes to quote brief passages in connection with a review written for inclusion in a magazine, newspaper, or broadcast.

Cataloging-in-Publication Data on file with the Library of Congress.

ISBN 0-89526-017-4

Published in the United States by
Regnery Publishing, Inc.
An Eagle Publishing Company
One Massachusetts Avenue, NW
Washington, DC 20001

Visit us at www.regnery.com

Distributed to the trade by
National Book Network
4720-A Boston Way
Lanham, MD 20706

Printed on acid-free paper

Manufactured in the United States of America

10 9

Books are available in quantity for promotional or premium use. Write to Director of Special Sales, Regnery Publishing, Inc., One Massachusetts Avenue, NW, Washington, DC 20001, for information on discounts and terms, or call (202) 216-0600.

To Anne O'Neill, the most courageous person I ever met—J.O.

For my wife, Monica, and my daughter, Alexis, whose love
makes life worth living—J.C.

CONTENTS

PREFACE

John O'Neill served in Coastal Division 11 in Vietnam, the same unit John F. Kerry had been assigned. When Kerry left Vietnam after a brief four months, O'Neill took over command of Swift Boat PCF 94, which Kerry had commanded. When O'Neill completed his one-year tour in Vietnam, he returned to the United States to find Kerry in a prominent position in the antiwar movement. O'Neill actively rebutted Kerry's accusations that war crimes were routinely being committed by the American military in Vietnam. In a now famous television debate in 1971, John O'Neill faced John Kerry on the *Dick Cavett Show*.

Jerry Corsi began studying political violence in the United States in the late 1960s. He would later receive a Ph.D. in political science from Harvard University. Corsi conducted two major studies on the Vietnam Veterans Against the War (VVAW) at Brandeis University's

Center for the Study of Violence. During this time, Kerry served as VVAW's national spokesman.

O'Neill and Corsi had been friends since their undergraduate years. While O'Neill was attending the Naval Academy, Corsi was studying at Case Western Reserve University, and the two competed against each other in intercollegiate debate. In 2004, when Corsi saw the O'Neill vs. Kerry debate on the *Dick Cavett Show* rebroadcast by C-SPAN, he telephoned his old friend. The two had not spoken in more than thirty years. After reconnecting, they decided to work together to write this book. Both strongly oppose John Kerry's 2004 candidacy for president of the United States.

INTRODUCTION

"I do not believe John Kerry is fit to be commander in chief of the armed forces of the United States. This is not a political issue. It is a matter of his judgment, truthfulness, reliability, loyalty, and trust—all absolute tenets of command."

REAR ADMIRAL ROY F. HOFFMANN, USN (RETIRED)

commander of the Swift Boats in Vietnam, 1968–1969
Call sign "Latch"

"To really understand John Kerry, you have to listen to those who served with him in Vietnam."

JOHN EDWARDS

vice presidential candidate of the Democratic Party

3

Swift Boat Veterans Reunion
Norfolk, Virginia
Summer 2003

After more than thirty years, the Swift Boat veterans have gathered for another reunion. They are veterans of PCFs (Patrol Crafts Fast), small aluminum boats the Navy procured early in the Vietnam War. Initially, they operated offshore to prevent enemy infiltration by sea. Later, the Navy sent these PCFs into the rivers and canals of Vietnam's Mekong Delta and into the U Minh and Nam Can forests to the south. These areas had been held by the North Vietnamese for a generation.

The reunion is a happy gathering of more than three hundred members and their spouses. It is a proud unit holding numerous individual medals and Presidential Unit Citations. This unit lost more than fifty souls in Vietnam.

The Swiftees are from all walks of life—admirals to aged hippies. They are from all parts of the nation, from all races, and from all political persuasions. They are united, however, by one common experience: service in Coastal Squadron One during the Vietnam War.

Dan Daly, the master of ceremonies, introduces the many dignitaries in attendance. They are received with polite applause. But the Swiftees who are introduced are met with cheers and the marked enthusiasm that characterizes their brotherhood. Despite the span of thirty years, the memories and nostalgia of long ago—sadness, death, joy, and friendship—have not been forgotten.

When it came time for Daly to recognize Senator John Kerry, present earlier that day, as the man "who may be the next president of the United States," deafening silence followed. Even a single clap would have sounded like a cannon. Daly, embarrassed, said, "I guess I laid an egg with that one."

Kerry had made a cameo appearance accompanied by a film crew and a corps of directors and assistants at an earlier outdoor event. Pushing aside various Swiftees, Kerry positioned himself dockside so he could be filmed on the restored PCF that was the centerpiece of the reunion. As was his habit, Kerry ignored many of his fellow Swiftees. He placed himself front and center for the camera shot, pushing aside Swiftees like Jack Chenoweth, an officer and one of the true heroes of the "Rassmann" incident—which we will discuss in due course, and which Kerry later lied about in a $50 million ad campaign.

One of Kerry's political aides singled out some Swiftees to participate in his video. Most declined. After filming the cameo and allowing one or two snapshots to be taken dockside, Kerry and his entourage disappeared, not bothering to attend a memorial service for the Swiftees who had died in Vietnam. To many, Kerry's conduct at the 2003 reunion seemed exactly in character. Kerry's service in Vietnam had been devoted largely to his own self-interest at the cost of comradeship, honor, and tradition. So his staging a self-promotion video while ignoring a memorial service for dead comrades was not surprising. That day, the Swiftees wondered whether the nation would ever be told about the real John Kerry, the Kerry of Vietnam and the Kerry who led Vietnam Veterans Against the War.

Swift Vets for Truth Press Conference
Washington, D.C.
May 4, 2004

Nearly a year later, another gathering of the Swiftees occurred. Led by their former commanding officer in Vietnam, Rear Admiral Roy Hoffmann, the Swiftees had written an open letter to John Kerry. This letter, which is reprinted in the Appendix, revealed that Kerry had misrepresented his service in Vietnam and lied about his claims of atrocities committed as a matter of policy by his unit and the American military. The letter labeled Kerry a liar and a fraud, unfit to be the commander in chief of the United States Armed Forces—especially now, in a time of terrible challenge to the nation. Remarkably, about 200 Swiftees signed the letter. Fewer than 10 percent of those contacted declined to sign or indicated any support for Kerry's presidential campaign. The signers of the May 4, 2004, letter included almost every one of Kerry's commanders in Vietnam, fifteen of the twenty-three officers who served with him in An Thoi (where he claims to have been a hero), and a substantial majority of those who were with him during military operations.

At the press conference, eighteen signers rose one by one to the microphone and stated before the cameras why they opposed Kerry. The speakers included Kerry's former commander Grant Hibbard, who outlined Kerry's disingenuous application for the Purple Heart. Sailors Rich O'Mara, Steve Gardner, and Jim Steffes, who had served with Kerry, outlined his lies about purported war crimes in Vietnam. Officers such as Captain Bill Shumadine and Bob Elder were enraged by the falsehoods Kerry told about invented "atrocities" for his personal political gain once he had returned to the United States. Perhaps most moving was Joe Ponder, a disabled veteran who was badly wounded in a battle that Kerry's biography, *Tour of Duty*, wholly distorted, but which Ponder remembers vividly because of the battle wounds. Much of the pro-Kerry media, which routinely rotates a few token pro-Kerry veterans, simply ignored the press conference, focusing their attention instead on Kerry's new campaign aircraft and its technical components. Only C-SPAN covered the press conference honestly, broadcasting it in its entirety.

War Remnants Museum
Ho Chi Minh City
May 28, 2004

Shortly before Memorial Day 2004, wandering through Ho Chi Minh City, Bill Lupetti came upon the War Remnants Museum—formerly known as the War Crimes Museum. Lupetti, a Navy corpsman, had been stationed in Vietnam from 1969 through 1970 and had treated many wounded Swift vets. He was a corpsman at An Thoi, the same tiny base and unit in which both Kerry and O'Neill served. Lupetti had returned to Vietnam three decades later to try to piece together that part of his life and to learn whether his Vietnamese friends had survived the North Vietnamese takeover and resulting bloodbath.

In the museum, Lupetti found an exhibit dedicated to the world heroes whom the Vietnamese Communists credited with helping win the "resistance." Lupetti saw pictures of Chinese Communist leaders, banners from left-wing extremists groups worldwide, photos of American radicals from the 1960s, posters and photos from antiwar demonstrations around the world, and signs from terrorist groups such as Fatah (a PLO fringe group). Lupetti's gaze came to focus on one particularly large photograph and celebratory inscription. He realized that he had seen the face before—for the first time more than thirty years ago. It was John Kerry. The Vietnamese photo of a 1993 meeting of Kerry and Vietnamese leaders, including the General Secretary of the Vietnamese Communist Party Do Muoi, was to honor John Kerry's "heroic" contributions to the North Vietnamese victory.

Lupetti photographed the Kerry picture on the wall, went to an Internet café in Ho Chi Minh City, and immediately posted it on an online Swift Boat photo album maintained by Swiftees. It can be seen in www.WinterSoldier.com or in the photo pages of this book.

This sequence of events—the 2003 Swift Boat reunion, the Swift Boat Vets for the Truth press conference, and Bill Lupetti's discovery of the Kerry photo in the Communist war museum in Ho Chi Minh City—raises a series of questions that we hope to answer in this book.

What sort of combination of hypocrite and paradox is John Kerry? How can someone who, until recently, claimed he was a war criminal, who threw away his medals and supported the North Vietnamese with his words, who even met with enemy delegations in Paris while our soldiers were fighting and dying in the field, now switch sides to run as a hero of those he condemned as criminals in that war?

Why is Kerry's support among his fellow Swiftees limited to the handful of crewmen from his boat and a few others whom his campaign presents to the media? Why do an overwhelming majority of those who commanded or served with John Kerry oppose him? Why do the Vietnamese Communists single him out for a position of honor, while those who fought at his side so uniformly condemn him? Why do the Swiftees regard him as a man who would be a disastrous commander in chief?

Who is the real John Kerry, and why do we say he is unfit for command?

The answers to these questions are based on the testimony of many who served with Kerry or in his unit. We have probed the record of lies John Kerry advanced after he returned from Vietnam and served as the national spokesman for the radical Vietnam Veterans Against the War. It is our hope that the American people will consider this information in deciding Kerry's fitness to be commander in chief. His fellow veterans would have preferred to support a candidate from their small unit or, at the very least, to remain silent. But John Kerry's character and the Swiftees' duty to the American people, prevent that.

PART ONE

JOHN KERRY IN VIETNAM

ONE

DEBATING KERRY

John O'Neill

June 1971

In spring 1971, I was stationed at the Naval ROTC Unit at Holy Cross College in Massachusetts. After eight years away, I was desperate to return home to Texas. My father, a retired rear admiral, had suffered two heart attacks and was quite ill. Texas was also a place that I loved.

When I turned on the news that spring evening, I was sickened by what I saw—a broadcast of extracts from John Kerry's testimony in front of the Senate Foreign Relations Committee. He compared those of us who served in Vietnam to the army of Genghis Khan, committing war crimes such as rape and baby-killing "on a day-to-day basis with the full awareness of officers at all levels of command." I knew (as Kerry did) that he was lying about our Swift Boat unit and about the war in general. I was overwhelmed by the greatest sense of injustice that I had ever experienced—the memory of that night still haunts me today. I remembered my friends who served in Vietnam,

11

living and dead, from the Naval Academy and from Swift Boats, and how hard we had tried to avoid civilian casualties under terrible conditions, at considerable risk to ourselves. I remembered those wounded and killed on the Dam Doi river, some of whom I watched die, because we broadcast messages of hope and freedom, urging villagers (many of whom were held in these villages by the Viet Cong against their will) to Chu Hoi. Moving at slow speeds, we were sometimes shot at—and some of us died. I remembered the fighter pilots who had been killed or were captured because we used small planes and opted for precision bombing in Hanoi, Haiphong, and the North Vietnam river dikes, rather than massive, indiscriminate bombing with B-52s, as we had done in World War II. That night, I resolved that I would refute Kerry's lies.

John Kerry would like many people today to view his service in Vietnam as one of honor and courage. But the real John Kerry of Vietnam was a man who filed false operating reports, who faked Purple Hearts, and who took a fast pass through the combat zones. From the Revolutionary War to the present, politicians of both parties have attempted to garner political gain through association with wars and warriors. Kerry was another politician posing briefly as a warrior to acquire military credentials. His tour of Vietnam had been so very brief that he was disparagingly called "Quick John." He was rarely talked about when I was in Vietnam, but I had heard that he wounded himself and others with M-79 rounds, but I had never fully investigated that until spring 2004.

If John Kerry had just been another politician punching his ticket in the military, I wouldn't have cared. But for John Kerry to lie at the expense of his former comrades living and dead, in front of the Senate Foreign Relations Committee, just so he could outbid other radicals in the antiwar movement and gain attention was something else. Even his own crew members who now (after long persuasion) support him for president were "pissed" at the time. They "knew he was dead wrong," and their stomachs "turned" listening to Kerry speak and felt "disappointed and betrayed."[1] Millions of Vietnam veterans will never forget Kerry's spinning of lies—lies so damaging to his comrades but so profitable to himself.

I wrote to the Senate Foreign Relations Committee, which at the time was headed by antiwar activists like J. William Fulbright. Since I spent far longer than Kerry in Vietnam and had seen far more combat, I asked in my letter for a few minutes to reply to Kerry's lies and those of fellow purported antiwar Vietnam veterans. I received a letter in response, telling me that there was no room for another speaker. Nor was there room in most of the national media for any of the millions of us who felt differently from Kerry and his nine hundred radical "brothers"—many of them impostors who had never even been to Vietnam. Al Hubbard, the executive director of the Vietnam Veterans Against the War, while Kerry was the group's national spokesman, received far more coverage on all three networks as a "wounded fighter pilot" until it was revealed that Hubbard was a sergeant who had never served in Vietnam, claiming a back injury from basketball.

After Kerry's testimony in May 1971, I read a short piece by Bruce Kesler, in the *New York Times*. In this article, Bruce, then a young ex-Marine just returned from Vietnam, maintained that Kerry was not speaking for the majority of Vietnam veterans in his speeches criminalizing our troops. Bruce was an enlisted Marine from one of the toughest parts of Brooklyn. When I finally reached him, he invited me to a press conference held by the Vietnam Veterans for a Just Peace at the National Press Club. The purpose of the press conference was to counter Kerry's war-crimes charges and challenge him to debate. I met Bruce the day before the press conference in the Washington, D.C., YMCA, where the group (given its limited finances) was staying. This was a stark contrast to the Georgetown townhouse in which Kerry the revolutionary stayed while in Washington.

Our press conference was surprisingly well attended. In it, I identified Kerry as a member of my unit, and I challenged him to a debate. We got some coverage, although far less than Hubbard and Kerry's revolutionary band of VVAW activists did. I worked closely with Bruce and later spent a pleasant night or two with him and his gracious mother. Although our backgrounds could not have been more different, we share to this day a passionate love of human freedom, a dislike for totalitarian regimes of whatever stripe, and sickness and revulsion at the injustice of Kerry's lies.

The media has recently attempted to paint our efforts to debate Kerry as a Nixon plot. The media relies on self-serving comments by Nixon aides taking credit for our group's appearance. But the truth is that while we were supportive of Nixon's "peace with honor" withdrawal from Vietnam (as opposed to a pullout that would leave our POWs behind), we were largely Democrats or apolitical, and our principal assets, other than a few contributions, consisted of the money I had set aside for law school and Bruce's mother's telephone.

While I delivered companion speeches alongside Kerry at the National Conference of Mayors, he turned down numerous debate offers from CBS's *60 Minutes* and many other forums. Finally, Dick Cavett offered his show, which Kerry accepted because Cavett was a friend and shared his antiwar position.[2]

Tour of Duty and Kerry's spin machine have attempted to deflect attention from his disastrous performance in the *Dick Cavett Show* debate by claiming there was a plot by the Veterans of Foreign Wars, Charles Colson, or Richard Nixon. This is ridiculous. Kerry performed disastrously because he was lying about his war-crimes claim, and it was obvious to anyone, including the audience, which, as Dick

Cavett observed, was solidly on his side at the beginning but booing him at the end.

I did meet with Richard Nixon, and also with many Democratic representatives and members of Congress, such as Senator Henry "Scoop" Jackson and Congressman Olin Earl "Tiger" Teague, who encouraged me not to give up and to do my best. Unknown to me at the time, an actual tape and transcript of my meeting with Nixon are available today. The meeting begins with me telling President Nixon that although my family and I were Democrats who voted for Hubert Humphrey, we supported Nixon on the issue of a phased withdrawal from Vietnam. And I remember even now the gasps at the meeting following my comment and my vague feeling that I must have done something inappropriate.

Since the debate was proposed by Dick Cavett, who was on Nixon's "enemies" list and whose show was accepted by Kerry as a friendly forum, it is more than a little disingenuous to present Kerry's debacle as a Nixon or a VFW plot. I obviously did not need any encouragement from Nixon, Colson, Senator Jackson, or anyone else. I had plenty of encouragement from the fifteen or so of my friends labeled "war criminals" by Kerry and whose names are carved today in the dark V of the Vietnam Memorial. I continue to think of them often as young men who had bright futures, not simply names on a dark wall. I also received encouraging calls from many Swiftees, like my closest friend, Elmo Zumwalt III. I've always been proud that while Kerry wanted letters of support for him from members of our unit to wave against me in the debate, he was only able to get one such letter.

I debated Kerry on June 30, 1971. The debate received high ratings, and Cavett has recalled it as one of the most memorable of his distinguished shows.

While *Tour of Duty* seeks to present the show as a victory for Kerry, citing the only known article so stating, it was in reality a debacle for him and his radical VVAW buddies. Our respective home-town newspapers, the *Boston Globe* (Kerry's) and the *San Antonio Express* (mine), agreed that Kerry had suffered a heavy loss. And in the White House, people were thrilled.[3] Much more important to me than politicos or newspapers were my fellow Vietnam veterans, Swiftees, and the widows and children of my friends who had died in Vietnam. All of them thought that I had won the debate. In 1977, I was partic-ularly proud to be thanked by Lieutenant General John Flynn who learned of the debate after his release. A senior U.S. POW in Vietnam, he had been confronted while in captivity with Kerry's war-crimes charges. To the audience that mattered to me, I won.

When the debate opened, I concentrated primarily on these war-crimes charges. They were far more important than the geopolitical opinions of two young vets, one of whom had been in Vietnam for only four months. I ended my opening statement by quoting Oscar Wilde's *The Ballad of Reading Gaol*:

And all men kill the thing they love, . . .
The coward does it with a kiss,
The brave man with a sword!

For me, that quotation summed all I knew then and know now of John Kerry—a self-promoted war hero who in reality was the greatest moral coward I had ever met, willing to sell out friends and comrades for political fame. Kerry's response was "Wow. Well, there are so many things really. . . . " I was surprised because I realized that Kerry was not insulted by my comments. For him, our debate was simply another game of political calculation. The questions of right and wrong, good and evil, played no real role in his thinking; he simply said whatever sounded popular. Lying about his friends on one hand, or being called a moral coward on the other, had little impact on a person whose only values were political or ideological calculations. Fortunately, a videotape of the debate survives. Anyone who wishes to understand John Kerry should view it. You won't find it on Kerry's website, but it is available at www.WinterSoldier.com (transcript), C-SPAN, and other websites.

That day, I repeatedly asked Kerry to list any war crimes or atrocities committed in our unit, Coastal Division 11.[4] He named generalities such as harassment and interdiction fire zones (commonly known as "H&I fire zones") and free-fire zones. A free-fire zone in Vietnam was an area in which one had discretion to fire if enemy were sighted, without first checking with headquarters. It required restraint and was not a war crime. Likewise, H&I meant firing at enemy positions in order to secure passage, or in the case of the Ho Chi Minh trail, interdict supplies. None of these activities would be regarded by any normal military expert as a war crime then or now.

Shockingly, when I directly confronted him about our small unit, Coastal Division 11, and his claims of war crimes there by our comrades, Kerry essentially collapsed and was unable to list a single "personal atrocity," as he labeled it, that he had actually witnessed—a remarkable concession from the "King of the Vietnam Veterans as War Criminals." When face to face across a table with someone from exactly the same unit, Kerry could not come up with a single instance of any atrocity in our unit or that he himself had actually seen in Vietnam. The reason that he could not describe any atrocities was because there were no atrocities.

Near the end of the debate, and in a rare moment of departure from Dick Cavett's genuine effort to serve as an impartial moderator,

Cavett asked whether either of us believed in the "cliché" that a bloodbath would occur if the United States were to withdraw from Vietnam. I answered that I thought that there would be a bloodbath, given the assassinations that we saw in the Can Mau region and the executions by the Viet Cong of South Vietnamese soldiers whose bodies we recovered in rivers and canals. Kerry answered in substance that it would never occur, that at most there might be five thousand people killed—a number so small that it was "lunacy" to talk about it. Some 3.5 million people are estimated to have died in the Communist purges at the end of the Vietnam War, including the 2.5 million in the killing fields of Cambodia. In Laos, whole peoples were eliminated. There were 1.4 million refugees, many of whom made it to the United States. Tens of thousands of "boat people" perished at sea trying to escape. I often wonder if Kerry is haunted (as I am) by his answer and by the thought of those lost souls, who once loved and lived and experienced the joys of life, but whom he so casually dismissed that day.

In the opinion of a recent biography of Kerry, that debate marked Kerry's high-water mark for many years, and after the debate "as quickly as Kerry's star had risen, it began to fade." Other than a failed congressional run (a campaign that I had predicted in the debate and that Kerry had denied) in which Kerry lost a safe Democratic seat, he was not heard from again in politics for more than a decade.

After our debate, Kerry refused all future debates (although while accompanied by a VVAW mob, he did show up for a short prescheduled joint appearance in Boston).[5] I was more than happy to go home to law school.

Other than giving a speech during the 1972 Republican campaign, I have had almost no political involvement for over thirty years. Almost routinely every four years, many of my fellow Swiftees and I were asked to cooperate with the campaigns of Kerry's opponents—

liberal and conservative, Republican and Democrat. Like me, almost all Swiftees refused to get involved. We wanted to leave the past behind. But that changed when it became apparent that Kerry might actually become commander in chief.

I was in a recovery room in February 2004, having just donated a kidney to my wonderful wife, Anne, when I looked at the television screen and saw John Kerry—in a brown flight jacket (which we had never worn in Vietnam) surrounded by a small crew of PCF veterans used like token props, announcing a primary victory. We Swiftees began talking, and soon. Our old commander, Admiral Hoffmann—now seventy-eight and still using his call sign, "Latch"— was again organizing us.

John Kerry's name tossed around as "president" and "commander in chief" summoned many of us from long political slumber—from games with grandchildren or feet by the fire—to render one last service to the nation. That service is the hard task of informing an uninformed America—against the wishes of a media sympathetic to Kerry and his myth—of John Kerry's total unfitness to command our armed forces or lead our nation. We are our own small "band of brothers," resolved to sound the alarm.

THE RELUCTANT WARRIOR

"Kerry arrived in-country with a strong anti-Vietnam War bias and a self-serving determination to build a foundation for his political future."

REAR ADMIRAL ROY HOFFMANN, USN (RETIRED)

Swift Boat Veterans for Truth Press Conference
Washington, D.C., May 4, 2004

Some people believe that John Kerry's military record from some thirty-five years ago makes no difference as he runs for president in 2004. But Kerry's Vietnam record is important because Kerry himself says that it is important. And as the future commander in chief, it's important to the men and women of our Armed forces, and to our country in its War on Terror. Since 1972, Kerry has run a one-trick campaign for every office he has sought. His relatively short military service has been the basis and constant theme upon which he loudly and without reservation proclaims himself a "war hero." He is willing, if not eager, to contrast his supposed military accomplishments against the military records of his opponents, which he has repeatedly belittled with enthusiasm. Kerry spent more time in the 2004 campaign arrayed in a brown leather flight jacket (which we never wore in the ninety-degree heat of Vietnam) and in a variety of other uniforms at political rallies than he ever spent fighting in Vietnam.

Constantly surrounded by a small cast of veterans, opponent after opponent, issue after issue, Kerry runs on his short record of three combat months (plus one training month) in Vietnam thirty-four years ago. He has placed full-page campaign ads in the *New York Times* with photos of himself receiving a medal. He has spent nearly $50 million on a particularly fraudulent ad portraying Kerry the infantryman stalking unknown foes through the jungle, followed by two speeches from thirty-four years ago. In the 2004 campaign, Kerry has pursued the war-hero theme with a persistent purpose, repeatedly demeaning the purported nonexperience of his opponents, including his eight opponents in the Democratic primary, Vice President Dick Cheney, and of course, President George W. Bush. In the past, Kerry has consistently used the same theme to attack his political opponents: in 1972 against Roger Durkin during the Democratic primary for the congressional seat in Lowell, Massachusetts; in 1984 against liberal Democrat James Shannon in the Massachusetts senatorial race; in 1990 against Republican businessman James Rappaport during Kerry's senatorial reelection campaign; and in 1996 against Republican challenger and former Massachusetts governor William Weld, whom Kerry narrowly beat in a closely contested senate race. Every campaign since 1972 begins and ends with Kerry the "war hero" boasting about his limited and controversial military record as one of his chief qualifications for office.

Most veterans, even those with real war wounds and long histories of service under enemy fire, would find it bizarre to apply for any job on the basis of their war records. That someone with Kerry's record would do so is even more bizarre.

The Antiwar Recruit

John Kerry has often implied that he volunteered for the military right after college. But Kerry petitioned his draft board for a student deferment. At Yale, Kerry's antiwar political views were well known. He was chairman of the Political Union and used his commencement address in 1966 to criticize the foreign policy of President Lyndon Johnson, especially with regard to Vietnam. When he approached his draft board for permission to study for a year in Paris, the draft board refused and Kerry decided to enlist in the Navy.[1] The Navy or the Coast Guard were considered good choices for reluctant young men who figured they were doomed to be drafted. Sailors could get into combat, but the risk of being assigned combat duty was less likely because North Vietnamese and Viet Cong didn't have battleships, submarines, or aircraft carriers.

The top choice was the Navy Reserves where the duty commitment was shorter and a larger proportion of the period could be served stateside on inactive duty.

John Kerry's service record indicates that on February 18, 1966, he enlisted in the United States Naval Reserves, status "inactive," not in the U.S. Navy. These details are conveniently left out of all pro-Kerry biographies. Douglas Brinkley records that Kerry entered Officer Candidate School in Newport, Rhode Island; however, again he fails to note that Kerry was seeking to be an officer of the U.S. Naval Reserve.[2]

The First "Tour of Vietnam"

John Kerry's first year of duty, from June 1967 to June 1968, was spent aboard the USS *Gridley*, a guided-missile frigate. During this year, Kerry experienced no combat. His assignment on board the *Gridley* is, however, the basis on which Kerry claims to have served "two tours" in Vietnam. Kerry's 2004 presidential campaign describes his service in the following words, which frequently get picked up uncritically by the news media: "After graduating from Yale, Kerry enlisted in the Navy and was sent to Vietnam in 1967. He served two tours of duty and won a Bronze Star, a Silver Star, and three Purple Hearts." A closer examination of his service record, however, shows that the assignment in 1967 was not to Vietnam, but to the *Gridley*. The guided-missile frigate was in the Pacific and in December 1967 did guard duty for planes operating in the China Sea and the Gulf of Tonkin. To say that Kerry was sent to Vietnam in 1967 exaggerates what was actually service on a deep fleet ocean vessel, involving no combat. Indeed, from June 1967 to November 1967, the *Gridley* operated along the California coast, and on January 2, 1968, the *Gridley* sailed for Australia and then returned to Long Beach, California on June 8. In other words, the *Gridley* was in what could be considered a "fighting zone" (still far off the coast of Vietnam) for probably fewer than five weeks while Kerry was aboard; five weeks off the coast of Vietnam could hardly be called a "tour in Vietnam."

Captain James F. Kelly Jr., USN (retired), Kerry's executive officer on the *Gridley*, remembers Kerry as serious and mature. Kelly even tried to recruit Kerry into a Navy career. His regard for Kerry, however, ended when he learned of the young sailor's antiwar activities. Kelly recently wrote:

While [Kerry] was protesting against the war, many of us were still fighting it. Many of us felt betrayed that one of our own, a decorated hero, would give comfort to the enemy by such actions. Whatever one thinks of the wisdom of becoming involved in that war, two presidents—both Democrats—committed the armed forces they commanded to fight it.

And make no mistake; actions by the likes of [Jane] Fonda and Kerry were damaging to our morale, gave aid and comfort to the forces we were fighting, and altered the eventual outcome in a manner less favorable to the United States than if they had kept their mouths shut. The time for antiwar protests is before the war starts.[3]

Like so many military veterans and most of Kerry's later Swift comrades, Captain Kelly, some thirty-five years later, still has no doubt in his mind that John Kerry's "antiwar activities while our troops were still fighting, dying and being tortured in filthy Vietnam prisons were despicable." For this reason, Kelly has refused to support his ex-shipmate in his campaign to become commander in chief of the United States military forces.

The Swift Boat "Volunteer"
Mid-November 1968 to March 17, 1969

The Navy first brought Swift Boats to Vietnam in 1966 to control the coast of Vietnam. The high-speed, 50-foot boats were specifically designed to intercept and inspect all offshore traffic. In addition, they carried mortars to provide offshore fire support. Swift Boats had no armor, and relied solely on their speed and firepower. Each boat had a six-man crew, and the boats operated in small divisions around Vietnam. In the early days, Swifts saw infrequent combat, which is apparently why they attracted Kerry.

Kerry volunteered for service on the Swifts and was selected. Given his extreme opposition to the Vietnam War and his view that it was an immoral enterprise, Kerry's action has always puzzled most Swiftees. But according to a Kerry biography written by *Boston Globe* reporters, Swift Boats were considered safe at the time: "Kerry also believed a swift boat assignment would keep him away from the frontlines of combat." Indeed, Kerry confirms it himself: "At the time, the boats had very little to do with the war," he wrote in his 1986 contribution to *The Vietnam Experience: A War Remembered.* "They were engaged in coastal patrolling and that's what I thought I was going to be doing. Although I wanted to see for myself what was going on, I didn't really want to get involved in the war."[4]

In late 1968, the Swift Boat mission was redefined to root out the enemy hiding in the difficult terrain of the canals and rivers of the Mekong Delta—much more dangerous service for the unarmored Swift Boats. Kerry's voluntary sojourn off the relatively pleasant coast would end. Later, when he was ordered into real combat, he strenuously objected, according to various Swift officers.

Commander Grant Hibbard, USN (retired), Kerry's first commander in Coastal Division 14, put the point succinctly: "Kerry told everybody that he was going to be president one day—you know, the next JFK from Massachusetts. Maybe he just thought Swift Boats would be a safe PT-109."[5]

William Franke, a Swift Boat veteran from Coastal Division 11, where Kerry would be assigned after his training at Cam Ranh Bay, had similar feelings about Kerry:

Some amongst us further object to what we consider to be Kerry's belligerent disrespect for duty and the military. While in Vietnam, Kerry was an outspoken critic to the point of being characterized by some as a perpetual whiner. He was constantly objecting to the war, stating that the U.S. had no business being there and the missions were not something that military forces should be engaged in. He objected that he had to serve in the canals, repeatedly demanding to be transferred back to the much safer duty of coastal patrol. He objected to the various operations, complaining that they were poorly thought out. He objected to the performance of the officers who were his senior, asserting that these missions were only designed to gain fame and career advancement for them.

On November 17, 1968, Kerry arrived in Vietnam and reported for duty to Coastal Squadron One, Coastal Division 14, at Cam Ranh Bay in South Vietnam. Cam Ranh, a French tourist town with a well-protected deep-water harbor and wide, beautiful white beaches, was generally regarded as the safest place in Vietnam. For this reason, American presidents visiting Vietnam would often stay there. Kerry spent one month of his four-month Vietnam tour training in Cam Ranh Bay.

Interestingly, from his very first days in Vietnam, Kerry kept a journal that he showed to no one. One of his first Vietnam entries involves what he called "a cruel little game."[6] In this antiwar entry, Kerry described a fisherman quaking with fear while being interrogated by the division commander and several officers. Kerry wrote that they kept running "their index fingers across their throat." According to Grant Hibbard, the division commander, and other Cam Ranh officers, this entry is a complete lie. The officers involved in this story could not speak Vietnamese, and prisoners were turned over to Vietnamese military authorities for interrogation.

Since the beginning of his tour, Kerry had a habit of wildly exaggerating his experience in his journal and in his accounts of his experience. Cam Ranh was a safe place, and being an officer in training was hardly exciting. In letters home, Kerry invents a nonexistent adventure that he repeats in *Tour of Duty*. He explains that after a few patrols in rough water at Cam Ranh, officers "come back pissing red and that several people have broken bones." None of the Swiftees from Cam Ranh remember any incident of this kind. Division commander Grant Hibbard brands it a lie, since there were no records or memory of any such incident in the year that Kerry was there.

These exaggerated entries in his journal would serve as the basis of Kerry's Vietnam stories for the next thirty years. The theme of these stories is almost always the same: Kerry portrays himself as a noble war hero who has no choice but to struggle mightily against the many military villains who surrounded him from the top down in the United States Army and Navy.

Kerry has refused to execute Standard Form 180, which would release to the public all his military and medical records.[7] He has not done so despite the demands of more than 250 of his fellow veterans. Kerry has also refused to publicly release his Vietnam journal or the totality of his films and photos from Vietnam. He has allowed a peek at those records only to his biographer, Douglas Brinkley, and journalists he considers friendly. Moreover, only a doctor selected by the campaign has been allowed to view Kerry's medical records.

But, as we'll see, there's a lot to discover about Kerry's military service.

THREE

THE PURPLE HEART HUNTER

"Many took exception to the Purple Hearts awarded to Kerry. His 'wounds' were suspect, so insignificant as to not be worthy of the award of such a medal. That Kerry would seek the Purple Heart for such 'wounds' is a mockery of the intent of the Purple Heart and an abridgement of the valor of those to whom the Purple Heart had been awarded with justification."

WILLIAM FRANKE

Swift Boat veteran

A normal tour of duty in Vietnam was at least one year for all personnel. Many sailors, like Tom Wright (who would later object to operating with Kerry in Vietnam) and Steven Gardner (the gunner's mate who sat behind and above Kerry for most of his Vietnam stay and came to regard him as incompetent and dishonest), stayed for longer periods either because of the special needs of the Navy or because they had volunteered to do so. With very few exceptions in the history of Swift Boats in Vietnam, everyone served a one-year tour unless he was seriously wounded. One exception was John Kerry, who requested to leave Vietnam after four months, citing an obscure regulation that permitted release of personnel with three Purple Hearts. John Kerry is also the only known Swiftee who received the Purple Heart for a self-inflicted wound.

None of Kerry's Purple Hearts were for serious injuries. They were concededly minor scratches at best, resulting in no lost duty time. Each Purple Heart decoration is very controversial, with considerable evidence (and in two of the cases, with incontrovertible and conclusive evidence) that the minor injuries were caused by Kerry's own hand and were not the result of hostile fire of any kind. They are a subject of ridicule within our unit. "I did get cut a few times, but I forgot to recommend myself for a Purple Heart. Sorry about that," wrote John Howland, a boat commander with call sign "Gremlin."[1]

Moreover, many Swiftees have now come forth to question Kerry's deception. "I was there the entire time Kerry was and witnessed two of his war 'wounds.' I was also present during the action [in which] he received his Bronze Star. I know what a fraud he is. How can I help?" wrote Van Odell, a gunner from Kerry's unit in An Thoi.[2] Commander John Kipp, USN (retired), of Coastal Division 13 also volunteered, "If there is anything I can do to unmask this charlatan, please let me know. He brings disgrace to all who served."

Swiftees have remarked that, if Kerry faked even one of these awards, he owes the Navy 243 additional days in Vietnam before he runs for anything. In a unit where terribly wounded personnel like Shelton White (now an undersea film producer who records specials for *National Geographic*) chose to return to duty after three wounds on the same day, Kerry's actions were disgraceful. Indeed, many share the feelings of Admiral Roy Hoffmann, to whom all Swiftees reported: Kerry simply "bugged out" when the heat was on.

For military personnel no medal or award (with the exception of the Congressional Medal of Honor) holds the significance of the Purple Heart. John O'Neill remembers witnessing, as a five-year-old child, the presentation of the Purple Heart to his widowed aunt, standing with her five children, at a memorial service for his uncle, a fighter pilot lost in Korea. Many remember the Purple Heart pinned on the pillows of the badly wounded in military hospitals throughout the world during America's wars in defense of freedom. For this reason, there were those in Coastal Division 11 who turned down Purple Hearts because, when the medals were offered, these honorable men felt they did not really deserve them. Veteran Gary Townsend wrote, "I was on PCF 3 [from] 1969 to 1970...I also turned down a Purple Heart award (which required seven stitches) offered to me while in Nam because I thought a little cut was insignificant as to what others had suffered to get theirs."[3]

To cheat by getting a Purple Heart from a self-inflicted wound would be regarded as befitting the lowest levels of military conduct. To use such a faked award to leave a combat sector early would be lower yet. Finally, to make or use faked awards as the basis for running for president of the United States, while faulting one's political opponents for not having similar military decorations, would represent unbelievable hypocrisy and the truly bottom rung of human conduct. Anyone engaging in such conduct would be unfit for even the lowest rank in the Navy, to say nothing of the commander in chief.

The Purple Heart Adventure in the Boston Whaler

JOHN KERRY'S STORY

John Kerry's website presents his first Purple Heart incident in typical heroic fashion: "December 2, 1968—Kerry experiences first intense combat; receives first combat related injury."[4]

As Kerry described the situation to Brinkley, who recounts the event in *Tour of Duty*, he grew bored in his first two weeks in Vietnam while awaiting the assignment of his own boat. So he volunteered for a "special mission" on a boat the Navy calls a skimmer but which Kerry knew as a "Boston whaler." The craft was a foam-filled boat, not a PCF Swift Boat. Kerry and two enlisted men were patrolling that night, as Kerry described it, "the shore off a Viet Cong–infested peninsula north of Cam Ranh." Kerry claims that he and his two crew members spent the night being "scared shitless," creeping up in the darkness on fishermen in sampans. They feared that the fishermen in sampans with no lights might be Viet Cong.

According to Kerry, the action started early in the morning, around 2 or 3 a.m., when it was still dark. Here are Kerry's words, quoted by Brinkley:

The jungle closed in on us on both sides. It was scary as hell. You could hear yourself breathing. We were almost touching the shore. Suddenly, through the magnified moonlight of the infrared "starlight scope," I watched, mesmerized, as a group of sampans glided in toward the shore. We had been briefed that this was a favorite crossing area for VC trafficking contraband.[5]

Kerry reports that he turned off the motor and paddled the Boston Whaler out of the inlet into the bay. Then he saw the Vietnamese pull their sampans onto the beach; they began to unload something. Kerry decided to light a flare to illuminate the area.

The entire sky seemed to explode into daylight. The men from the sampans bolted erect, stiff with shock for only an instant before they sprang for cover like a herd of panicked gazelles [Kerry] had once seen on TV's "Wild Kingdom." We opened

fire... The light from the flares started to fade, the air was full
of explosions. My M-16 jammed, and as I bent down in the boat
to grab another gun, a stinging piece of heat socked into my arm
and just seemed to burn like hell. By this time one of the sailors
had started the engine and we ran by the beach, strafing it. Then
it was quiet.[6]

That was the entire action. As Kerry explained to Brinkley, he was
not about to go chasing after the Vietnamese running away. "We
stayed quiet and low because we did not want to illuminate ourselves
at this point," Kerry explains.

In the dead of night, without any knowledge of what kind of
force was there, we were not all about to go crawling on the
beach to get our asses shot off. We were unprotected; we didn't
have ammunition; we didn't have cover; we just weren't prepared for that.... So we first shot the sampans so that they were
destroyed and whatever was in them was destroyed.[7]

In the introduction of the incident in the book, Kerry said that it
"was a half-assed action that hardly qualified as combat, but it was
my first, and that made it exciting." Kerry and his crew loaded their
gear in the Swift Boat that was there to cover them, and with the
Boston Whaler in tow, they headed back to Cam Ranh Bay. Brinkley
ends his discussion by quoting Kerry's summary, an account that
again paints a larger-than-life picture:

"I felt terribly seasoned after this minor skirmish, but since I
couldn't put my finger on what we had really accomplished or
on what had happened, it was difficult to feel satisfied," Kerry
recalled. "I never saw where the piece of shrapnel had come

from, and the vision of the men running like gazelles haunted me. It seemed stupid. My gunner didn't know where the people were when he first started firing. The M-16 bullets had kicked up the sand way to the right of them as he sprayed the beach, slowly walking the line of fire over to where the men had been leaping for cover. I had been shouting directions and trying to unjam my gun. The third crewman was locked in a personal struggle with the engine, trying to start it. I just shook my head and said, 'Jesus Christ.' It made me wonder if a year of *training* was worth anything." Nevertheless, the episode introduced Kerry to combat with the VC and earned him a Purple Heart.[8]

THE *Boston Globe's* ACCOUNT

A somewhat different version is recounted in the Kerry biography written by the *Boston Globe* reporters. In this account, Kerry had emphasized that he was patrolling with the Boston Whaler in a free-fire curfew zone, and that "anyone violating the curfew could be considered an enemy and shot."[9]

By the time the *Globe* biography was written, questions had been raised about whether the incident involved any enemy fire at all. The *Globe* reporters covered this point as follows:

> The Kerry campaign showed the *Boston Globe* a one-page document listing Kerry's medical treatment during some of his service time. The notation said: "3 DEC 1968 U.S. NAVAL SUPPORT FACILITY CAM RANH BAY RVN FPO Shrapnel in left arm above elbow. Shrapnel removed and apply Bacitracin dressing. Ret to duty."

The *Globe* asked the campaign whether Kerry was certain that he received enemy fire and whether Kerry remembers the Purple Heart being questioned by a superior officer. The campaign did not respond to those specific questions and, instead, provided a written statement about the fact that the Navy did find the action worthy of a Purple Heart.[10]

The two men serving alongside Kerry that night had similar memories of the incident that led to Kerry's first wartime injury. William Zaldonis, who was manning an M-60, and Patrick Runyon, operating the engine, said they spotted some people running from a sampan to a nearby shoreline. When they refused to obey a call to stop, Kerry's crew began shooting. "When John told me to open up, I opened up," Zaldonis recalled. Zaldonis and Runyon both said they were too busy to notice how Kerry was hit. "I assume they fired back," Zaldonis said. "If you can picture me holding an M-60 machine gun and firing it—what do I see? Nothing. If they were firing at us, it was hard for me to tell."

Runyon, too, said that he assumed the suspected Viet Cong fired back because Kerry was hit by a piece of shrapnel. "When you have a lot of shooting going on, a lot of noise, you are scared, the adrenaline is up," Runyon said. "I can't say for sure that we got return fire or how [Kerry] got nicked. I couldn't say one way or the other. I know he did get nicked, a scrape on the arm."[11]

In a separate conversation, Runyon related that he never knew Kerry was wounded. So even in the *Globe* biography accounting, it was not clear that there was any enemy fire, just a question about how Kerry might have been hit with shrapnel.

The *Globe* reporters noted that, upon the group's return to base, Kerry's commander, Grant Hibbard, was very skeptical about the injury. The *Globe* account also quoted William Schachte, the officer in command for the operation. As the *Globe* reporters recount, Another person involved that day was William Schachte, who oversaw the mission and went on to become an admiral. In 2003, Schachte responded: 'It was not a very serious wound at all.'[12]

Still, on Sunday, April 18, 2004, when NBC correspondent Tim Russert questioned Kerry on national television about the skimmer incident, Kerry described the incident as "the most frightening night" of his Vietnam experience. The *Globe* reporters noted that Kerry had declined to be interviewed about the Boston Whaler incident for their book. Kerry's refusal to be interviewed may well have been because witnesses such as Commander Hibbard, Dr. Louis Letson, Rear Admiral William Schachte, and others had begun to surface, and Kerry's fabricated story of "the most frightening night" had begun to unravel.

WHAT REALLY HAPPENED

The truth is that at the time of this incident Kerry was an officer in command (OinC) under training, aboard the skimmer using the call sign "Robin" on the operation, with now-Rear Admiral William Schachte using the call sign "Batman," who was also on the skimmer. After Kerry's M-16 jammed, Kerry picked up an M-79 grenade launcher and fired a grenade too close, causing a tiny piece of shrapnel (one to two centimeters) to barely stick in his arm. Schachte berated Kerry for almost putting someone's eye out. There was no hostile fire of any kind, nor did Kerry on the way back mention to PCF OinC Mike Voss, who commanded the PCF that had towed the skimmer, that he was wounded. There was no report of any hostile fire that day (as would be required), nor do the records at Cam Ranh Bay reveal any such hostile fire. No other records reflect any hostile fire. There is also no casualty report, as would have been required had there actually been a casualty.

Following "the most frightening night" of his life, to the surprise of both Schachte and the treating doctor, Louis Letson, Kerry managed to keep the tiny hanging fragment barely embedded in his arm until he arrived at sickbay a number of miles away and a considerable time later, where he was examined by Dr. Letson. Dr. Letson, who has never forgotten the experience, reported it to his Democratic county chairman early in the 2004 primary campaign. When Kerry appeared at sickbay, Dr. Letson asked, "Why are you here?" in surprise, observing Kerry's unimpressive scratch. Kerry answered, "I've been wounded by hostile fire." Accompanying crewmen then told Dr. Letson that Kerry had wounded himself. Dr. Letson used tweezers to remove the tiny fragment, which he identified as shrapnel like that from an M-79 (not from a rifle bullet, etc.), and put a small bandage on Kerry's arm.

The following morning Kerry appeared at the office of Coastal Division 14 Commander Grant Hibbard and applied for the Purple Heart. Hibbard, who had learned from Schachte of the absence of hostile fire and self-infliction of the "wound" by Kerry himself, looked down at the tiny scratch (which he said was smaller than a rose thorn prick) and turned down the award since there was no hostile fire.[13]

When we interviewed Grant Hibbard for this book, he was equally emphatic that Kerry's slight injury, in his opinion, could not possibly merit the Purple Heart:

Q: When did you first meet John Kerry?
GH: Kerry reported to my division in November 1968. I didn't know him from Adam.

Q: Can you describe the mission in which Kerry got his first Purple Heart?
GH: Kerry requested permission to go on a skimmer operation with Lieutenant Schachte, my most senior and trusted lieutenant, using a Boston Whaler to try to interdict a Viet Cong movement of arms and munitions. The next morning at the briefing, I was informed that no enemy fire had been received on that mission. Our units had fired on some VC units running on

the beach. We were all in my office, some of the crew members,
I remember Schachte being there. This was thirty-six years ago;
it really didn't seem all that important at the time. Here was
this lieutenant, junior grade, who was saying "I got wounded,"
and everybody else, the crew that were present were saying, "We
didn't get any fire. We don't know how he got the scratch."
Kerry showed me the scratch on his arm. I hadn't been informed
that he had any medical treatment. The scratch didn't look like
much to me; I've seen worse injuries from a rose thorn.

Q: Did Kerry want you to recommend him for a Purple Heart?
GH: Yes, that was his whole point. He had this little piece of
shrapnel in his hand. It was tiny. I was told later that Kerry had
fired an M-79 grenade and that he had misjudged it. He fired it
too close to the shore, and it exploded on a rock or something.
He got hit by a piece of shrapnel from a grenade that he had fired
himself. The injury was self-inflicted, that's what made sense to
me. I told Kerry to "forget it." There was no hostile fire, the
injury was self-inflicted for all I knew, besides it was nothing
really more than a scratch. Kerry wasn't getting any Purple
Heart recommendation from me.

Q: How did Kerry get a Purple Heart from the incident then?
GH: I don't know. It beats me. I know I didn't recommend him for
a Purple Heart. Kerry probably wrote up the paperwork and recommended himself, that's all I can figure out. If it ever came across
my desk, I don't have any recollection of it. Kerry didn't get my
signature. I said "no way" and told him to get out of my office.[14]

Amazingly, Kerry somehow "gamed the system" nearly three
months later to obtain the Purple Heart that Hibbard had denied.

How he obtained the award is unknown, since his refusal to execute
Standard Form 180 means that whatever documents exist are known
only to Kerry, the Department of Defense, and God. It is clear that
there should be numerous other documents, but only a treatment
record reflecting a scratch and a certificate signed three months later
have been produced. There is, of course, no "after-action" hostile fire
or casualty report, as occurred in the case of every other instance of
hostile fire or casualty. This is because there was no hostile fire, casualty, or action on this "most frightening night" of Kerry's Vietnam
experience. Dr. Louis Letson agreed with Grant Hibbard. Kerry's
injury was minor and probably self-inflicted:

> The incident that occasioned my meeting with Lieutenant Kerry
> began while he was patrolling the coast at night just north of
> Cam Ranh Bay where I was the only medical officer for a small
> support base. Kerry returned from that night on patrol with an
> injury.
>
> Kerry reported that he had observed suspicious activity on
> shore and fired a flare to illuminate the area. According to Kerry,
> they had been engaged in a firefight, receiving small arms fire
> from on shore. He said that his injury resulted from this enemy
> action.
>
> The story he told was different from what his crewmen had
> to say about that night. Some of his crew confided that they did
> not receive any fire from shore, but that Kerry had fired a
> grenade round at close range to the shore. The crewman who
> related this story thought that the injury was from a fragment of
> the grenade shell that had ricocheted back from the rocks.
>
> That seemed to fit the injury I treated.
>
> What I saw was a small piece of metal sticking very superfi-
> cially in the skin of Kerry's arm. The metal fragment measured

about one centimeter in length and was about two or three millimeters in diameter. It certainly did not look like a round from
a rifle. I simply removed the piece of metal by lifting it out of the
skin with forceps. I doubt that it penetrated more than three or
four millimeters. It did not require probing to find it, nor did it
require any anesthesia to remove it. It did not require any
sutures to close the wound. The wound was covered with a
band-aid. No other injuries were reported and I do not recall that
there was any injury to the boat.

Lieutenant Kerry's crew related that he had told them that he
would be president one day. He liked to think of himself as the
next JFK from Massachusetts. I remember that Jess Carreon was
present at the time and he, in fact, made the entry into Lieutenant Kerry's medical record.[15]

Both Hibbard and Letson wondered why Kerry had even bothered
to go to the dispensary. Kerry's report of the injury as a combat injury
seemed at best to be exaggerated. The crewmen present maintained
that there was no evidence of enemy fire, and their conclusion was
that Kerry had been hit by a fragment of his own grenade.

Kerry's proponents have also pointed to a fitness report for Kerry
that was filed by Hibbard rating Kerry "excellent" as proof that
Kerry's service in Cam Ranh was unusually good. In reality, the Kerry
fitness report (which leaves fourteen of the eighteen categories,
including "integrity," marked "unobserved") is a marginal report.
Hibbard has stated that he wished to provide in the report a mediocre
evaluation without permanently destroying Kerry, given his short
four-week period of evaluation. At the time the report was made, Hibbard did not know of Kerry's later-finagled first Purple Heart.

Most Swiftees who were with Kerry at Cam Ranh Bay never knew
until Kerry decided to run for president that he had somehow

successfully maneuvered his way to this undeserved Purple Heart. But in Kerry's own unit, Coastal Division 14, his attempt to gain the award through fraud marked him as someone who could never be trusted. When Kerry was dispatched to go to An Thoi with Lieutenant Tedd Peck (now Captain, USNR, retired), Peck told him, "Kerry, follow me no closer than a thousand yards. If you get any closer, I'll teach you what a real Purple Heart is."

A Trip to An Thoi

In contrast to the pretty beaches and placid existence at Cam Ranh Bay where Kerry was stationed, Coastal Division 11 was engaged in a gritty struggle against a North Vietnamese base area, deep in the mangrove swamps in the extreme south and west of Vietnam. This area, commonly known as the U Minh and Nam Can forests, had been under North Vietnamese control since the 1940s and was used for POW camps. Most POWs never left these camps. The city of Nam Can, one of the few free outposts in the area, had been overrun by the North Vietnamese in February 1968. Swift operations in the area were supported from an offshore outpost at An Thoi, located on an island off the coast.

The ultimate commander of United States Naval and Coast Guard forces in Vietnam, Admiral Elmo "Bud" Zumwalt III developed a strategy—with enthusiastic support of then-Captain Roy Hoffmann—to use underutilized offshore naval assets to rip control of area waterways from the North Vietnamese. His model was the Mississippi River campaigns of the Civil War, which had effectively used specialized craft.

Zumwalt was deeply admired by almost all Swiftees. A hero in World War II, Zumwalt was also later known as the man who brought women to the Naval Academy and into full participation in the Navy.

He was also recognized as a crusader against racism. Zumwalt was a visionary whose sponsorship of missile ships and other innovations mark today's Navy. He also often rode into danger with the Swiftees. Kerry's later charge on *Meet the Press* in April 1971 that Zumwalt and others were war criminals cut deeply at the heart of Swiftees. Perhaps part of Kerry's unjustifiable attack on Zumwalt was motivated by the fact that it was Zumwalt's decision to use Swift Boats on dangerous riverine missions that ended with Kerry's hopes of avoiding action.

THE DINNER THAT NEVER HAPPENED
Kerry's Fictitious Journal Account

In Kerry's account of the An Thoi transfer, he makes up an entire conversation with the skipper of the landing ship tank (LST) who Kerry claims invited him and Peck for dinner on their way to An Thoi. As Kerry told the story in *Tour of Duty*, the LST captain launched into a discussion about his role in what had become known as the "Bo De massacre." According to the version of the story told by Kerry, the LST captain presented a defensive account, attempting to correct a *Stars and Stripes* story criticizing him for LST covering fire that had supposedly fallen short, exposing Swiftees on the mission to unnecessary casualties.

But according to Captain Peck's recollection and that of Kerry's crewman Steven Gardner, he and Kerry were at the LST only a few minutes for refueling, not enough time for a comfortable dinner with the LST captain—and there was no conversation about "the massacre" as described by Kerry. Even more significant, Kerry's account of the "Bo De massacre" is a breathtaking lie. In *Tour*, Kerry presents the first Swift incident on the Bo De as a "massacre" of Swiftees with seventeen wounded caused by the incompetence of all commanders whom he chose to blame rather than the vagaries of war or the enemy. Kerry's fabrication comes even though he was not there. Joe Ponder was there as a Swiftee on the mission in question. Today, still badly disabled and on crutches from the incident, Ponder says, "There were only three persons wounded—not seventeen as Kerry states— and I was the first. I do not understand his criticism of our officers. I've always been proud of our officers."

Ponder maintains today that the person who truly shamed and offended him was John Kerry, whose fraudulent account of war crimes in *Tour of Duty* has led his own grandchildren to ask him, "Did you commit the war crimes John Kerry describes?" At the press conference held by the Swift Boat Veterans for Truth in Washington, D.C., on May 4, 2004, Ponder was in tears, not from his wounds or the agony of standing with his braces, but from the wounds that Kerry's lies in *Tour of Duty* had left upon his heart and his family.

THE BRIEF ASSIGNMENT IN AN THOI: KERRY'S VERSION

As Kerry has admitted in *Tour of Duty*, he was ordered against his will to Coastal Division 11 in An Thoi in December 1968. Tedd Peck recalls Kerry's constant griping about the transfer. In *Tour of Duty*, Brinkley writes that both Kerry and Peck were opposed to their assign- ment. Following Kerry's account, Brinkley quotes Peck telling his men, "There was no way I was leaving Cam Ranh Bay voluntarily to go up the rivers. That was a suicide mission."[16] Brinkley relates a tor- tured explanation of why Kerry was finally forced to accept the assign- ment: He claims that he missed one of the division meetings held to solicit volunteers because he was at the Air Force PX. Peck remem- bered Kerry distinctly objecting, saying that he had not volunteered for the war that was occurring in the Nam Can and U Minh forests. Peck believed that Kerry did not belong in the Navy. In Brinkley's account, the one guy who got Peck's ire up the quickest was John

Kerry, who he found standoffish and condescending. "I didn't like anything about him," Peck proclaimed, "Nothing." For his part, Kerry liked Peck, and decades later recalled none of this supposed animosity between them.[17]

At any rate, Kerry's time at An Thoi was short. Within a week, Kerry and the crew of PCF 44 were on their way to the less hazardous CosDiv 13, at Cat Lo. Kerry has tried to make it appear that he was disappointed at being so quickly reassigned from An Thoi. Here is the account he gave to biographer Douglas Brinkley:

> "I tried to fight the change—not because we wanted to stay in An Thoi and be shot at, but because we didn't want to have to move and resettle again," Kerry noted. "Our mail was already lost, and the trip back against the monsoon seas promised to be nothing but a bitch. It was just that."[18]

THE REAL REASON KERRY WAS REASSIGNED

When they got to An Thoi, Kerry continued to object to his placement in this dangerous assignment against his will, so much so that he was given routine offshore patrols not involving any possibility of action until Coastal Division 11 could figure out a way to get rid of him. Within a week, Kerry was transferred to Coastal Division 13, headquartered near the former French resort town of Vung Tau. While Coastal Division 13 had been involved in substantial action, it was less than what Kerry avoided by his transfer. What his fellow Swiftees concluded was that Kerry had a very high regard for his own well-being and very little nerve for facing serious combat.

According to Peck, it was simply easier to get Kerry out of An Thoi than to have to listen to his constant bellyaching about how he had not volunteered for this kind of danger. Better just to get rid of Kerry and let him be somebody else's problem.

William Franke echoes Tedd Peck's explanation of why Kerry was so quickly transferred out of An Thoi:

> Kerry vigorously protested being transferred to An Thoi, arguing that he had volunteered only for coastal patrol and not for the far more hazardous duty of missions within the inland water-ways. Indeed, his objections were so strong that, upon his first assignment to An Thoi, he was transferred out within a week.[19]

So off Kerry went to Cat Lo, where the patrols were on wider, less dangerous rivers than the treacherous canals of the U Minh forest and Cau Mau peninsula.

Christmas In "Cambodia"
Vietnam, December 1968

JOHN KERRY'S STORY

If there is one story told over and over again by John Kerry since his return from Vietnam, it is the heart-wrenching tale of how he spent Christmas Eve and Christmas Day illegally in Cambodia. From the early 1970s, when he used the tale as part of his proof for war crimes in Cambodia, through the mid-1980s and the 1990s, Kerry has spoken and written again and again of how he was illegally ordered to enter Cambodia.

On the floor of the U.S. Senate on March 27, 1986, Kerry launched one of his many attacks against President Reagan—this time charging that President Reagan's actions in Central America were leading the United States into yet another Vietnam, claiming that he could recognize the error of the administration's ways because he had experienced firsthand the duplicity of the Nixon administration in lying

about American incursions into Cambodia during the Vietnam War.
Kerry charged that he had been illegally ordered into Cambodia during Christmas 1968:

> I remember Christmas of 1968 sitting on a gunboat in Cambo-
> dia. I remember what it was like to be shot at by the Vietnamese
> and Khmer Rouge and Cambodians, and have the president of
> the United States telling the American people that I was not
> there; the troops were not in Cambodia. I have that memory
> which is seared—seared—in me.[20]

Kerry also described, for example, for the *Boston Herald* his vivid
memories of his Christmas Eve spent in Cambodia:

> I remember spending Christmas Eve of 1968 five miles across
> the Cambodian border being shot at by our South Vietnamese
> allies who were drunk and celebrating Christmas. The absurdity
> of almost being killed by our own allies in a country in which
> President Nixon claimed there were no American troops was
> very real.[21]

As recently as July 7, 2004, Michael Kranish of the *Boston Globe*
repeated Kerry's Christmas in Cambodia story on FOX News Chan-
nel's *Hannity & Colmes*, indicating that it was a critical turning point
in Kerry's life. Kranish had no knowledge, even after his extensive
study of Kerry, that he was simply repeating a total fabrication by
Kerry. And Kranish was right: Study of the Christmas in Cambodia
story is central to understanding John Kerry.

The story is also in the pages of the 2004 biography written by
Krahish and other *Boston Globe* reporters. As we have come to

expect, the story is twisted at the end to provide justification for yet another of Kerry's political ruses, this time used to justify what Kerry portrays as his noble and continuing distrust of government pronouncements:

> To top it off, Kerry said later that he had gone into Cambodia, despite President Nixon's assurances to the American public that there was no combat action in this neutral territory. The young sailor began to develop a deep mistrust of the U.S. government pronouncements, he later recalled.[22]

Even without minimal investigation, a critical press should have been able to spot the story as a total fabrication: Richard Nixon did not become president of the United States until twenty-six days after John Kerry's Christmas in Cambodia.

WHAT REALLY HAPPENED: CHRISTMAS IN VIETNAM

Despite the dramatic memories of his Christmas in Cambodia, Kerry's statements are complete lies. Kerry was never in Cambodia during Christmas 1968, or at all during the Vietnam War. In reality, during Christmas 1968, he was more than fifty miles away from Cambodia. Kerry was never ordered into Cambodia by anyone and would have been court-martialed had he gone there.

During Christmas 1968, Kerry was stationed at Coastal Division 13 in Cat Lo. Coastal Division 13's patrol areas extended to Sa Dec, about fifty-five miles from the Cambodian border. Areas closer than fifty-five miles to the Cambodian border in the area of the Mekong River were patrolled by PBRs, a small river patrol craft, and not by Swift Boats. Preventing border crossings was considered so important at the time that an LCU (a large, mechanized landing craft) and several PBRs were stationed to ensure that no one could cross the border. A large sign at the border prohibited entry. Tom Anderson, Commander of River Division 531, who was in charge of the PBRs, confirmed that there were no Swifts anywhere in the area and that they would have been stopped had they appeared.

All the living commanders in Kerry's chain of command—Joe Streuhli (Commander of CosDiv 13), George Elliott (Commander of CosDiv 11), Adrian Lonsdale (Captain, USCG and Commander, Coastal Surveillance Center at An Thoi), Rear Admiral Roy Hoffmann (Commander, Coastal Surveillance Force Vietnam, CTF 115), and Rear Admiral Art Price (Commander of River Patrol Force, CTF 116)—deny that Kerry was ever ordered to Cambodia. They indicate that Kerry would have been seriously disciplined or court-martialed had he gone there. At least three of the five crewmen on Kerry's PCF 44 boat—Bill Zaldonis, Steven Hatch, and Steve Gardner—deny that they or their boat were ever in Cambodia. The remaining two crewmen declined to be interviewed for this book. Gardner, in particular, will never forget those days in late December when he was wounded on PCF 44, not in Cambodia, but many miles away in Vietnam.

The Cambodia incursion story is not included in *Tour of Duty*. Instead, Kerry replaces the story with a report about a mortar attack that occurred on Christmas Eve 1968 "near the Cambodia border" in a town called Sa Dec, some fifty-five miles from the Cambodian border.[23] Somehow, Kerry's secret illegal mission to Cambodia, which he recounted on the floor of the U.S. Senate in 1986, is now a firefight at Sa Dec and a Christmas day spent back at the base writing entries in his journal.

The truth is that Kerry made up his secret mission into Cambodia. Much like Kerry's many other lies relating to supposed "war crimes" committed by the U.S. military in Vietnam, the lie about the illegal Cambodian incursion painted his superiors up the chain of command—

men such as Commander Streuhli, Commander Elliott, Admiral Hoffmann, and Admiral Zumwalt, all distinguished Naval heroes and men of integrity—as villains faced down by John Kerry, a solitary hero in grave and exotic danger and forced illegally and against his will into harm's way.

The same sorts of lies were repeated over and over in Kerry's anti-war book, *The New Soldier*, a book filled with preposterous, false confessions of bogus war crimes committed by the participants (who were often not even real veterans) against their will and under orders from dishonest superiors. Kerry's Christmas in Cambodia typifies the sort of lie upon which Kerry has built a false persona and a political career.

The story of Christmas 1968 has one final chapter. When refueling his PCF near Dong Tam, Kerry and his crew were told that the Bob Hope USO show was at the Dong Tam base. So Kerry decided to leave his station on the river and go searching for the Bob Hope Christmas show. Unable to find the show, he risked boat and crew by unknowingly blundering into one of the most dangerous canals in Vietnam, a canal that to those who knew the area was notorious for Viet Cong ambushes. Given the easy navigation by radar and map of the rivers involved—not much more difficult than driving a car—Kerry had just performed a feat of reverse navigation worthy of Wrong Way Corrigan.

There is, of course, no record that Kerry ever informed anyone of what he did, where he was, or where he was going—all required by regulations for the safety of the boat and crew. He did, however, record the Bob Hope adventure in his journal so he could be sure to share it in *Tour of Duty*.[24]

FOUR

WAR CRIMES

"Kerry seemed to believe that there were no rules in a free-fire zone and you were supposed to kill everyone. I didn't see it that way. I will tell you in all candor that the only baby killer I knew in Vietnam was John F. Kerry."

WILLIAM FRANKE

Swift Boat veteran, Coastal Division 11

John Kerry invented a "war hero" persona in his private journals and in the home movies he filmed and staged in Vietnam. Playing the lead role, he developed a past intended to advance his future political ambitions. In reality, Kerry was regarded by his military peers as reckless with human life. While the Brinkley biography recalls that he used the call sign Square Jaw for a short time in Vietnam, it doesn't mention the sign he actually used for most of his tour: Boston Strangler.[1] Kerry portrays himself as an officer constantly protesting to his superiors about criminal war policies and inappropriate tactics. In reality, while Kerry constantly complained about the location of his assignments to his peers, he hardly ever said a word of protest or spoke out in objection to any superior officer.

Only after returning home did Kerry argue publicly that war crimes were committed on a daily basis at the direction of all levels of command. He compared his superior officers to Lieutenant Calley of My Lai infamy. Kerry's accusations of war crimes typically relied on impostors posing as veterans who concocted incidents that, when investigated, proved to be exaggerations or fabrications. On the other hand, the propriety of Kerry's own conduct in Vietnam was and is the subject of serious question.

The following are incidents that took place in An Thoi where Kerry was reassigned after Cat Lo. They have been reported to the authors by those who witnessed the ruthlessness of Kerry's conduct toward the Vietnamese people. In these incidents, Kerry's behavior (concealed from higher commanders by his own fraudulent reports) was in direct violation of orders promulgated by Admiral Elmo Zumwalt specifically designed to prevent oppression of the Vietnamese. These orders are filed in the archives of Texas Tech University.

In this chapter we also review several fictitious incidents Kerry reported in his journal and narrated in *Tour of Duty*. These incidents involved occasions when he imagines himself confronting superiors with antiwar sentiments and objections to military policies he felt were inappropriate. But these conversations never happened. Kerry invented them to create the false impression that he was an outspoken critic of the war and war policies while in Vietnam. The reality was that Kerry was always deferential to his superiors and that he limited his criticism to his peers or to the private pages of his journal.

The evidence shows that John Kerry was a ruthless operator in the field with little regard for life.

The Sampan Incident

January 1969

JOHN KERRY'S STORY

Kerry recounts that both his and another Swift Boat, PCF 21, were patrolling at night and continually running aground. Biographer Douglas Brinkley drew his account of what happened from Kerry's journals and his subsequent explanations:

> The night was pitch-black, neither Swift's search or boarding lights were working properly, and both boats kept getting stuck on the bottom of the shallow channel. "Many minutes of silent patrolling had gone by when one of the men yelled, 'Sampan off the port bow,'" Kerry wrote. "Everybody froze and we slowed the engines quickly. But the sampan was already by us and wasn't stopping. It was past curfew and nothing was allowed in the river. I told the gunner to fire a few warning shots and in the confusion all guns opened up. We moved in on the sampan, and taking one of the battle lanterns off the bulkhead shone it on the silhouette of the craft that was now dead in the water."[2]

Critical in this account is Kerry's statement that he ordered the gunner to fire "a few warning shots." In the next sentence Brinkley records Kerry's self-justification of the action, one of many different versions that he would subsequently offer to make the actions he took seem part of standard operating procedure:

> Technically, the two PCFs had done nothing wrong. The sampan, operating past curfew, was undeniably in a free-fire zone; what's more, there had been more than a few instances of

sampans trying to get close enough to U.S. Navy vessels to toss bombs into their pilothouses.[3]

In other words, Kerry is trying to establish that opening fire on the sampan was justified—a preemptive attack in self-defense. For Kerry, it was critical to maintain that his actions were taken according to Navy policy; otherwise, he had no defense. A Nuremberg defense— "just following orders"—was and is Kerry's chosen line. Kerry then admitted the civilian casualties he caused:

> But knowing that they were following official Navy policy didn't make it any easier to deal with what the crews saw next. "The light revealed a woman standing in the stern of the sampan with a child of perhaps two years or less in her arms," Kerry wrote. "Neither [was] harmed. We asked her where the men from the stern were, as one of the gunners was sure that he had seen someone moving back there. She gesticulated wildly and I could see traces of blood on the engine mounting. It was obvious that they had been blown overboard. Then somebody said there was a body up front and we moved in closer to see the limbs of a small child limp on the stacks of rice. She had already covered it, and when one of the men asked me if I wanted it uncovered I said no, realizing that the face would stay with me for the rest of my life and that it was better not to know whether there was a smile or a grimace or whether it was a girl or boy."[4]

Coastal Division 11 personnel recall at least two different explanations given for the action by Kerry—in addition to his excuses that it was the crew's fault and that it was a free-fire zone at the time. Kerry has suggested that, under the rice on the sampan, there might have been a bomb that could have been thrown into the Swift Boat had Kerry allowed the sampan to move close enough. Additionally, Kerry has suggested that the Viet Cong used women and children to cover their actions, and that there could have been Viet Cong in the boat ready to fire on them when they got closer. Another of Kerry's suggestions was that the woman might have been hiding weapons in the sunken boat, and he did not know if he and his crew were facing a real threat. These are strange explanations, since Kerry also admits that during his "entire stint in Vietnam, he never found a single piece of contraband on the hundreds of vessels he searched."[5]

Critically important is the fact that Kerry filed a phony after-action operational report concealing the fact that a child had been killed during the attack on the sampan and inventing a fleeing squad of Viet Cong. An operational report for this incident is one of the important missing documents that Kerry neglects to make public on his campaign website.

THE *BOSTON GLOBE'S* DISCOVERY

The Kerry biography written by the *Boston Globe* reporters cites a January 20, 1969, report of "a similar-sounding incident" involving an attack by Kerry and his crew on a sampan:

> In any case, while Kerry said in a 2003 interview that he wasn't sure when the boy in the sampan was killed, a Navy report says a similar-sounding incident took place on January 20, 1969. The crew of No. 44 "took sampan under fire, returned to capture 1 woman and a small child, one enemy KIA [Killed in Action]... believe four occupants fled to beach or possible KIA."

Kerry was the skipper of PCF 44 at the time. The Kerry campaign was sent a copy of the report, did not respond when asked if it matched Kerry's memory of the night the child was killed.[6] The

Globe reporters, who unknowingly uncovered a critical piece of evidence, were skeptical that there could have been two such incidents.

EYEWITNESS STEVE GARDNER

Gunner Steve Gardner sat above Kerry on the double .50-caliber mount that night in mid-January 1969. The PCF 44 boat, engines shut off, lay in ambush near the western mouth of the Cua Lon River. The boat's own generator was operating and its radar was on, with Kerry supposedly in the pilothouse monitoring the radar. Although the radar was easily capable of picking up the sampan early, Kerry gave no warning at all to the crew about the impending sampan and did not come out of the pilothouse. Instead, first an engine noise and then a sampan suddenly appeared in front of the boat—still no Kerry. The PCF lights were thrown on—still no Kerry. The boat was ordered to stop by the young Gunner Gardner—still no Kerry. There was no order, according to Gardner, to fire warning shots, as Kerry claimed. Indeed, there was no Kerry until it was over. When an occupant of the sampan appeared to Gardner to reach for or hold a weapon, he opened up (as did others), killing the father and, unintentionally, a child. Then Kerry finally appeared; he ordered the crew to cease fire and then threatened them. In this incident, Kerry's failure to pick up the sampan on radar is hard to understand. Harder still to understand is his absence as the officer in charge during the critical part of the episode.[7]

The fog of war can obscure anyone's vision, but there would certainly have been an inquiry at An Thoi to determine what happened and how a small child could have been inadvertently killed. The inquiry would have focused on why the sampan was not detected early and why normal measures like a flare or small-caliber warning shot were not used. To be fair, it is likely that the purpose of such an inquiry would not be to fix blame on anyone, but to avoid future miscalculation. And the major questions would have been: Where was Kerry? Why was there no warning? Why was a gunner's mate making the critical life-and-death decision instead of the officer in charge? Why the many different accounts by Kerry?

Kerry avoided any problem by filing an after-action report in which the dead child simply disappeared from the record and was replaced by a fleeing squad of Viet Cong, some likely killed by Kerry. A terrible human tragedy was converted by another Kerry lie into another sterling triumph by the young war hero.

According to Gardner, Kerry threatened to court-martial those involved, even though the crew believed they had seen weapons on the sampan. Gardner strongly believes that the sight of potential weapons justified the firing. When writing their biography of Kerry, the *Boston Globe* reporters note that pro-Kerry supporters have tried to discredit Gardner and dismiss his criticism of Kerry.

In March 2004, Gardner was quoted publicly for the first time about his views on Kerry in the *Boston Globe* and on *Time* magazine's website. But in the *Time* article, written by Douglas Brinkley, Kerry was quoted as reacting strongly to Gardner's criticism of him, saying that Gardner had "made up" stories. Brinkley dismissed Gardner, a supporter of President Bush, as being motivated by "one word: politics." Kerry said he couldn't remember the court-martial threat. Gardner denied the allegation that politics had anything to do with his comments. "Absolutely not," he said, saying that he has kept his feelings about Kerry to himself for thirty-five years and responded only when a *Globe* reporter tracked him down.[8]

Division Commander George Elliott never knew of the small child's death because all he received from Kerry was the false report, which found its way up the chain of command. The Commander Coastal Surveillance Force Vietnam (CTF 115) Quarterly Evaluation Report of March 29, 1969, states "...20 January PCFs 21 and 44 operating in An Xuyen Province...engaged the enemy with a resultant GDA of

one VC KIA (BC) [body count], four VC KIA (EST) and two VC CIA
(VQ 810650/44)." This is Kerry's victory—killing five imaginary Viet
Cong, capturing two Viet Cong in action (an exaggeration of the
mother and baby who were actually rescued from the sampan), and
simply omitting the dead child. It typified Kerry's "victories" in Vietnam—those of a master with a pen and paper and of gaming a system
of naval reporting built on trust. Admiral Hoffmann, receiving Kerry's
false report of probably killing five Viet Cong and capturing two others, sent him a congratulatory message. Upon learning of what Kerry
had actually done, Hoffmann recently expressed his contempt for
Kerry as a liar, false warrior, and fraud.

Despite Kerry's written report, rumors of the incident circulated
for years. The vivid memory of the small bloody sampan haunts Silver Star winner Bill Franke, a veteran of many battles. A boat officer
of Coastal Division 11 (and one of the real heroes of the incident portrayed in Kerry's "no man left behind" video), Jack Chenoweth has
recently written that "[t]he only atrocity I ever knew of or heard
about was Kerry killing the small child in the junk."[9]

In *Tour of Duty*, Kerry, according to one of his own accounts,
appears to have lost control of his boat after crazily ordering that
"warning shots" be fired at a small sampan with heavy .50-caliber
weapons, instead of the numerous small-caliber weapons on board.
According to the biography written by the *Boston Globe* reporters,
Kerry simply butchers a small sampan in a free-fire zone because it
would have been dangerous to approach.

The crews on the boats of Coastal Division 11, like law enforce-
ment officers in the United States approaching a stopped car on a
darkened highway, faced potential danger. Yet, thousands of sampans
were approached and boarded by Coastal Division 11 sailors without
causing the deaths of civilians, despite the fact that a great number of
these sampans were encountered in the dark of night in free-fire

zones. A free-fire zone was not an order to fire but was discretion to fire first if threatened by or when confronting enemy forces. There was always an apprehension of danger in approaching a junk or a sampan in the dark, but none of the Swiftees (so far as is known) would ever open fire because of fear that "a satchel" might be thrown. If Gardner's account is wrong and the above Kerry version is correct, it would have been simply butchery to open fire on a small sampan merely because it was in a free-fire zone.

Numerous Coastal Division 11 Swiftees recall the Cua Lon River sampan debacle with true distaste for Kerry, remembering him as someone who lied and who pushed the envelope of accepted conduct. Many Swiftees believe that Kerry was reckless with human life when the lives in question were Vietnamese. A statement from Swift Boat officer Bill Franke makes this point:

> The Vietnamese were, pursuant to martial laws enacted by the South Vietnamese government, not permitted to transit up the waterways from dusk until dawn. Under the Rules of Engagement, if a Swift Boat encountered such a boat under way during this prohibited time, and if that boat sought to flee, it was permissible to fire upon that boat.
>
> In virtually every instance, such a boat was simply returning late from fishing. Fishing was the means of survival for most of the Vietnamese. Absent clear indications of danger, Swift Boat crews simply did not open fire upon such boats. Rather, the vessel would be boarded, searched, and let go with a warning. Often the crew would notch the boat with a K-Bar knife, along the starboard gunnels just aft of the bow. If a boat with several such notches was stopped, the Officer-in-Charge might go so far as to fire a round from an M-16 into the hull, causing a leak that could be readily plugged but sending a message to the crew.

Kerry chose not to honor this code. Rather, when encountering a fishing boat returning up the river to a nearby village, Kerry's boat opened fire on the vessel. Whether one believes in Kerry's or Gardner's version, Kerry's boat was ultimately responsible. The fishing vessel could not possibly escape given the vast disparity in speed between sampans and Swift Boats. Franke writes:

"A Swift Boat carries three .50-caliber machine guns, two M-60 machine guns, and various other armaments. When, for example, the twin .50-caliber guns in the gun tub are discharged, it is a vicious, savage act. Eleven hundred rounds per minute scream into the darkness, for up to a mile, destroying anything in their path. No officer who honored this code would unleash such a savage attack upon a defenseless family absent clear and present danger."[10]

Tom Wright, another PCF commander, gave serious reflection to the way Kerry chose to interpret free-fire zones:

We believed that "free-fire" zones placed the greatest responsibility on the OinC because he alone had to decide if he was going to shoot. In the other areas, the ROE [rules of engagement] told you what to do. John Kerry thought that "free-fire" meant "kill anyone you see . . ." Not every person is a good combat commander. John Kerry was not a good combat commander.

In free-fire zones, you had to always consider your unit's safety and then the overall picture. Fire discipline was important. Your reputation was important. You wanted the enemy to see you as a competent, effective force that dominated his location. Shooting at someone just because you saw them was a mistake. We were trying to gain control over an area. To achieve that, we had to control the people in an area. I felt that being able to apprehend, question, and release a person in a free-fire zone was a major victory. The more we could communicate with the people, the more we could control their actions. We wanted them to accept us and our authority.

It was necessary to shoot in the free-fire zones from time to time and the circumstances normally fell within the normal ROE. Occasionally, at night or [in] poor visibility, we might shoot a little quicker than the Rules would have allowed, or engage a target based on secondary information. I always knew that I was responsible for the safety of my men and our actions. Working in a free-fire zone made me feel more responsible, not less.[11]

Wright had such difficulty working with Kerry that he finally objected to going on patrol with him:

John Kerry's leadership and operational style were different from mine. I can see how his crew thought he was a hero, but it seemed like he was a hero fighting out of situations he shouldn't have been in to begin with. I had a lot of trouble getting him to follow orders. Most specifically, I believed that overall responsibility rested squarely on the shoulders of the OTC/OinC in a free-fire zone. You had to be right and you had to have fire discipline. You couldn't blame something on the rules of engagement. I had some very serious problems with Kerry one day and I told the DivCom that I did not want Kerry in my group anymore.[12]

No discussion of this incident can be found on Kerry's campaign website, nor is there any official document among those Navy service records that Kerry has made public. Steve Gardner's testimony and the CTF 115 Quarterly Report both indicate that Kerry's boat picked up the woman and her baby who survived the debacle, whom Kerry's after-action report described as captured Viet Cong. Yet no record indicates what became of the woman or the child when Kerry's boat returned to shore. The squad of four Viet Cong fleeing to shore that existed only in Kerry's imagination and in his written report does not exist in *Tour*, or in Kerry's statements to Kranish, or in Kerry's secret journal, or in any recollection of anyone. Kerry's victory exists only in Kerry's mind. Nonetheless, he succeeded in pulling off this fraud until the recent record comparison.

Animal Slaughter

George Bates, an officer in Coastal Division 11, participated in numerous operations with Kerry from January 1969 through March 1969. In Bates's view, Kerry was a coward who overreacted with deadly force to protect himself when he felt threatened. Bates, a retired Navy captain, believed that Kerry treated the South Vietnamese in an almost criminal manner.

Bates is haunted by a particular patrol with Kerry on the Song Bo De River in the first part of 1969. With Kerry in the lead, the boats approached a small hamlet with three to four grass huts. Pigs and chickens were milling around peacefully. As the boats drew closer, the villagers fled. There were no political symbols or flags in evidence in the tiny village. It was obvious to Bates that existing policies, decency, and good sense required the boats to simply move on.

Instead, Kerry beached his boat directly in the small settlement. Upon his command, the numerous small animals were slaughtered by heavy-caliber machine guns. Acting more like a pirate than a naval officer, Kerry disembarked and ran around with a Zippo lighter, burning up the entire hamlet.

Bates has never forgotten Kerry's actions and was appalled by the complete hypocrisy of Kerry's quick shift to the role of a peace activist condemning war crimes upon his return. Even today, Bates describes Kerry as a man without a conscience.

Fabricated Protests Against War Crimes

In contrast to his highly questionable activities in combat and on patrol, Kerry invented an elaborate persona in his journal and the years after his tour, in which he repeatedly protested to his superiors against possible war crimes at great risk to his career.

Take, for example, Kerry's discussion of a meeting on January 22, 1969, in which Admiral Elmo Zumwalt addressed the Swift Boat commanders of Coastal Divisions 11 and 13. Kerry's journal reflects questions that he supposedly asked, critical of Operation Sealord. This event is reprised in *Tour of Duty*:

> "I asked how, if our job was ostensibly interdiction of the movement of supplies, they could justify offensive actions such as we had been sent on—attempts to draw the enemy into ambush and then destroy his ambush capability. He said that the purpose was to show the American flag—an answer that seemed very strange to me when I considered it was the Vietnamese flag that we were supposed to be fighting for. Why didn't we show their flag, or better yet let them run up the rivers and show their flag? Many friends of mine in the Marines told me about their operational orders and necessity for artillery wherever they go. The admiral went on to say that he knew Navy men found it hard to go out and find the enemy, but that the Army did it all the time and that we should get used to it. I wanted to point out that the Army was equipped and trained differently than us and that they had some form of support beyond that which we had, but then I thought better of it and silence was the better part of valor.

After some parrying, the admiral was finally rescued by his trusty aide Captain Roy Hoffmann, who stood up and made a few remarks about the unavoidability of innocent people being killed in Southeast Asia. Zumwalt declared this normal—fortunes of war, as it were, and to be expected.[13]

Roy Hoffmann notes that Kerry's version of the meeting on January 22, 1969, as just another "Kerry-concocted lie." Hoffmann states:

> I was standing behind General Abrams and Admiral Zumwalt observing the audience reaction. I distinctly remember Kerry sitting separated several seats from the nearest associate and to the left of the speakers. He did not ask one question or otherwise participate in the dialogue.[14]

The confrontation as imagined and reported by Kerry is typically self-serving, designed to advance the idea that he was an outspoken critic of military policy, willing to challenge his superiors whenever possible. Most of those in Coastal Divisions 11 and 13 remember Kerry as deferential to superiors.

During the television debate with John O'Neill on the *Dick Cavett Show*, Kerry related to O'Neill and the world the threats of mutiny in which he supposedly participated while in the military:

> We were fighting the [free-fire] policy very, very hard, to the point that many of the members were refusing to carry out orders on some of their missions, to the point where crews were starting to mutiny, [to] say, "I would not go back in the rivers again."[15]

The *Boston Globe* reporters reject Kerry's assertion, however, in their report of the debate:

None of the swift boat sailors and officers who served with Kerry and were interviewed said they could recall a mutinous threat. Nor did Kerry's subsequent actions suggest he was gun-shy.[16]

From the entry in his journal in 1969, to his gross exaggeration on the *Dick Cavett Show*, and in numerous speeches up to and including the publication of his campaign biography in 2004, John Kerry has lied. There never was any documented instance of a mutiny in Coastal Division 11 or 13—the Swiftees carried out their appointed missions as ordered, pure and simple.

Commander George Elliott, Kerry's direct commanding officer at An Thoi (who stood up for Kerry in 1996 when he was accused of a war crime during a press conference), labels Kerry's "mutiny" and war protest complete fabrications, as do more than twenty other officers and sailors.

Tour of Duty repeats another falsified story in Kerry's journal, this time involving Kerry and Donald Droz (a Swift Boat hero killed in 1969, a month after Kerry left Vietnam). Supposedly, Kerry confronted Coast Guard Captain Adrian Lonsdale with a speech worthy of John Wayne:

But the Swift skippers pressed Lonsdale to fight harder for the support their missions needed. Kerry opted to implore him for a policy change one last time. "Sir, all we need is to give the men a little more of a chance," he began. "They're willing to fight because they're here and that's what they have to do, but they want to fight with some prospects of getting somewhere. Why can't we have some helos that are waiting, always on the ready for us, so that when we get fired on first, if we must, we can at least expect some support and hope to get some of the enemy and make them actually worry about what we are doing. That way we might be able to catch some of them, or get some weapons or something. We could at least have a reason for going in there."[17]

Lonsdale, according to Kerry, did not answer the question. Instead, he gave a variety of excuses to the effect that he was worried about his job and that he had no choice but to do what Hoffmann wanted done with regard to Operation Sealord. Once again, like the *Dick Cavett Show* mutiny story and the fictionalized speech at the Operation Sealord meeting, the speech Kerry supposedly delivered to Lonsdale is also a complete fabrication, delivered only in Kerry's imagination and recalled by neither Lonsdale nor Hoffmann. None of the many superior officers who dealt with Kerry on a daily or weekly basis can ever remember him giving any such speeches. In Kerry's journal entries, his moral principles were foremost, and he was determined to speak out to those misguided authorities above him. In reality, Kerry was critical, grumbling, and antiwar when he talked with his peers, but deferential when addressing his superiors. The only "speaking out" Kerry did to his superiors was in his mind or the pages of his private journal.

Kerry could not recall any "personal" atrocities in which his unit was involved when he appeared on the *Dick Cavett Show*. By 2004, however, his memory had improved remarkably. In *Tour of Duty*, Brinkley writes:

Kerry would never forget how ardently Captain Hoffmann lauded the exploits of one "enterprising officer" from the Da Nang Swift division. The officer had surprised some thirty Vietnamese who were fishing in round, floating baskets just off the shore of a peninsula in an area that was, unfortunately for them, a free-fire zone. Hoffmann considered it ideal military thinking that the Swift skipper had shown the presence of mind to sneak his boat in between the baskets and the shore, cutting the fishermen off from escape and then opening fire on them. All the baskets were sunk, and so were the fishermen. "Fantastic," Hoffmann reportedly proclaimed upon hearing the news. Kerry himself would later hear Hoffmann praise such "industriousness" at a remarkable meeting in Saigon. Clearly, the Navy had undergone a sea change. Not only were cowboy antics on the rivers of Vietnam no longer frowned upon, they were rewarded with medals.

"I was in-country after this happened," Wade Sanders later wrote. When the OinCs heard about this, and heard that the butcher was being considered for a Silver Star, a howl or outcry was heard all the way to Cam Ranh Bay and Captain Hoffmann reversed the consideration of a medal. We all thought the son of a bitch should have been court-martialed."[18]

Wade Sanders, however, is a political friend of Kerry's who never served in Da Nang and was not in Vietnam at the time of the supposed incident. Sanders did receive a political appointment in the Clinton administration, with Kerry's help and was a contributor to Kerry's now-discredited 1971 book, *The New Soldier*, although Sanders does not here repeat the unsubstantiated allegations of war crimes made in the book. So Sanders, while never having seen the incident and never having any military service in Da Nang, states that although he was in-country only after the incident happened, he nonetheless recalls "hearing" about it. So Kerry relies upon the hearsay testimony of Wade Sanders, a longtime political operative in his debt, to support his claim.

This story is wholly denied by Admiral Hoffmann, who never worked on any medal recommendations in Vietnam, except one—the Medal of Honor that later went to Democratic senator Robert Kerrey of Nebraska—a genuine hero. It was simply not Hoffmann's job to award medals. In addition, numerous division commanders and Swiftees deny knowing anything about the purported incident. Moreover, neither Kerry nor Sanders (who were not officers in charge in Da Nang) ever observed or spoke to Hoffmann about the "incident."

The division commanders and many sailors strongly deny the basket story, and it is certain that there is neither a record nor any other known account of such an event. Since the officer in charge is not identified, nor are any details such as date, boats, or personnel provided, it is not possible to comment further on the alleged incident. So it is uncertain whether Kerry simply took an actual incident and distorted it to such a degree that it could no longer be recognized, or whether the incident was simply invented.

In 2003, the telephone rang at Admiral Roy Hoffmann's residence. It was John Kerry, calling shortly before his announcement that he was running for president. Hoffmann, who is now seventy-eight years old and who has survived sunken boats in both Korea and Vietnam and more hostile fire than nearly anyone among us, thought at first that the call was from Robert Kerrey, not John Kerry. Hoffmann, like most Swiftees, had never imagined that anyone would take John Kerry seriously as a contender for president of the United States. So for the first four or five minutes, Hoffmann responded enthusiastically, eager (as most Swiftees would be) to assist Robert Kerrey in his bid for the nation's highest office. Then, when Hoffmann realized he was speaking with John Kerry, not Robert Kerrey, his tone changed almost immediately and he became completely noncommittal. Once he declined to give Kerry his support, the conversation faded fast.

On March 15, 2004, Admiral Hoffmann's telephone rang again. Once again, the caller was John Kerry. Kerry had clinched the Democratic nomination, and he knew that Hoffmann was organizing Swiftees to bring out the truth about him, his exaggerated military record, and his antiwar lies that had slandered his fellow veterans. Kerry made the admiral an offer: If you will back off and drop your efforts, I will ensure that my biography, *Tour of Duty*, which I know is unfair to you, will be changed to make it accurate in a revised edition. Here is my secretary's number—you can get me anytime.

The offer from the Democratic presidential candidate was an attempt to flatter Hoffmann, a warrior whose coin is not power or wealth, but honor—an honor deeply impugned by Kerry's book. Hoffmann, after all, is a wounded survivor of the amphibious assault at Wonson, Korea, where his minesweeper still lies below the frigid waters of Wonson Harbor. Kerry knew that winning Hoffmann over to his side would thwart the Swiftees' efforts to discredit him. Hoffmann told Kerry that he and the vast majority of his shipmates could never forgive him for his defamation of our Navy and other U.S. Armed Forces by his slanderous and undocumented accusations of unspeakable atrocities in Vietnam before the U.S. Congress in 1971, his leadership in the VVAW, and his association with the traitorous Jane Fonda and others of her ilk. Surprisingly, Kerry responded by simply saying that he "was expressing his conviction."

If Admiral Hoffmann were truly a butcher whose conduct "sickens" John Kerry to this day, an impression one could easily gain from reading *Tour of Duty*, then why did he call Hoffmann to seek his support? Why would Kerry offer to change inaccuracies he knew were in *Tour of Duty* in exchange for Admiral Hoffmann and the Swiftees ceasing their activities? In e-mails on May 3, 2004, and on May 7, 2004, trying to dissuade Swiftees from joining Admiral Hoffmann, Wade Sanders referred to the group as "bitter drunks," something the sailors involved deeply resented. Moreover, Sanders referred to Joe Ponder, a seriously disabled Swiftee who cried when talking about Kerry's charges, as "a whining crybaby."

Why does it matter now that Kerry converted his own record from that of a ruthless, self-promoting liar hungry for medals and fame into that of an antiwar activist jeopardizing his career by protesting in imaginary conversations with superiors? Why does it even matter if he continues to do so today? It matters to the Swiftees because Kerry has libeled distinguished commanders such as Admiral Zumwalt and their fellow sailors, living and dead. More important, it matters deeply to the future of hundreds of thousands of servicemen and a nation that depends on its commander in chief for loyalty, support, stability, direction, and genuine care.

FIVE

MORE FRAUDULENT MEDALS

"Put me on the list...I was standing next to one of my crew at Seafloat when he was killed in a Sapper attack on the USS *Krishna* (Lanny Buroff 7/70). He was awarded the Navy Commendation Medal—posthumously. No Silver or Bronze Star like Kerry got for filling out forms."

DAVID BORDEN, PCF 40

April 28, 2004, e-mail

"As corpsman with the Marines (Golf 2/5) 1967–68, I agree totally with the information you are trying to get out on Kerry. Three Purple Hearts, Silver Star, Bronze Star in such a short tour is amazing...You will see Golf 2/5 was involved...in the battle for Hue City complete with block-to-block, house-to-house, and sometime room-to-room fighting. Throughout that battle and many others after that, I never saw anyone win so many decorations in such a short time. Actually, by the accounts I have read on the Silver Star, I would have punished him."

CORPSMAN JOHN "DOC" HIGGINS, U.S. MARINES (GOLF 2/5)

"When John Kerry got his third Purple Heart, we told him to leave. We knew how the system worked and we didn't want him in CosDiv11. Kerry didn't decide to manipulate the system to go home after four months; we asked him to go home."

THOMAS W. WRIGHT, USN (RETIRED)

Swift Boat commander

Far from his commercial portrayal as a purposeful warrior strolling boldly through the jungle, John Kerry was regarded by many Swiftees as a poor officer.

Tedd Peck, a Swift boat commander who operated with Kerry in Vietnam, asked Bill Zaldonis, a Kerry crewman and supporter, how he could possibly be in favor of Kerry. When Zaldonis replied that he wanted a warrior for president, Peck asked, "Yes, but who are you going to get?" Admiral Hoffmann characterized Kerry as a "loose cannon," while Captain Charles Plumly called him "devious, requiring constant supervision." For the mere three months that Kerry was involved in duty in Vietnam, he left behind an amazing legacy of Beetle Bailey bumbling. Steve Gardner is the sole crewman who was not swayed by Kerry during his many post-Vietnam years of solicitation aimed at gaining the support of his crew. Today, Gardner asks, "How can Kerry possibly be commander in chief when he couldn't competently command a six-man crew?" Gardner, a two-tour Swift Boat sailor who sat five feet behind Kerry in Vietnam and who saw many officers during his two years, judges Kerry to be by far the worst Swift Boat commander he saw in Vietnam:

Kerry was erratic. He hardly ever did what he was supposed to do. His command decisions put us in more peril then he should have. But mostly he just ran. When John Kerry looked out the bow of the boat and he saw tracer fire coming after him, he'd turn and run. That isn't what he was supposed to do. His job was to face into the fire, to quarter the boat so we could apply our twin .50-caliber machine guns on the enemy. That was our job in the canal, to stand our ground and suppress the enemy fire. All Kerry wanted to do was turn and "get out of Dodge" at the first sign of trouble. When he should have been fighting, calling in air support, he was hightailing it. That's always been my bone of contention with Kerry—his decision-making capabilities, that's what takes him out of contention as far as I'm concerned.[1]

While on patrol in one of the main rivers, for instance, Kerry ran his boat out of the water and aground for a number of hours—not particularly easy to do in the deep river channels. In *Tour of Duty*, James Wasser, another Kerry crewman (and a Kerry supporter), recounts one of Kerry's mishaps:

> In addition to leading the board-and-search operations, it was Wasser's responsibility to stand by his young skipper in the event Lieutenant Kerry committed a blunder. "Sometimes he got disoriented and misread the navigational maps," Wasser allowed. "It was easy to do. Once, we hit a sandbar and couldn't get loose. We didn't call in because we didn't want to get John in trouble. We just sat around for hours, waiting for high tide. It eventually came, and off we went."[2]

This, of course, left Kerry's boat almost defenseless, unable to maneuver, unable to bring guns to bear, unable to withdraw. Aground, Kerry's boat was totally vulnerable to mortar or any other type of attack. Kerry's mistake also left the area that his boat was supposed to be patrolling totally unguarded. Because of the boat's vulnerability and its inability to guard its patrol area and carry out its assignment on station, officers in charge of boats that ran seriously aground were required to report the situation to Coastal Division headquarters immediately. In the above incident, Kerry evidently chose not to call in to avoid getting "in trouble." While incidental minor grounding was seldom reported, a serious long-term grounding, like that of PCF 44 described above, would always have been reported, and very little trouble would have ensued given the nature of the brown-water navy. Kerry's decision not to report the episode to his superiors, based on fear of their disfavor, says much about him.

In addition to failing to report adverse occurrences, Kerry developed a reputation for simply wandering off aimlessly. For example, on one occasion, after being relieved, he simply diverted his boat into Saigon (now renamed Ho Chi Minh City by the Communists), "to taste the storied capital," without informing anyone that he had done so or where he was:

> Kerry asked the tactical operations man if there were any water-way restrictions on traffic to Saigon. Every night on patrol he gazed longingly upon the bright lights of the big city just seven miles away, as seductive as the City of Oz or Las Vegas glittering beyond the horizon. Saigon had boutiques, bars, black market deals, nightclubs, brothels, and fifty-six thousand registered prostitutes (plus who knows how many freelancers). There were some river-travel restrictions, the officer informed him, but then he confided that there were also a few loopholes, too. On the spot, Kerry decided to exploit those. The key was to have a plausible excuse at the ready should his boat be stopped on its way into the city. "We knew that while we were cruising up and down the river at night, someone was sitting at the bar of the

Majestic Hotel in the center of the city, drinking, probably with a girl at his side," Kerry explained. "It seemed wrong. We were jealous at any rate and wanted to share it. So instead of turning right as we left Nha Be after being relieved, we went left, up the Long Tau, and into the heart of the city. We didn't have permission from the division or anyone else, but we felt that we deserved an irresponsible, personal moment, so we did it anyway."[3]

Reading Brinkley's account, one wonders why Kerry chose to brag about being irresponsible to the point where he concocted ready-made excuses should he be stopped and questioned, just so he and his crew could share in the sin available in Saigon. Self-reported self-indulgence is hard to comprehend.

On March 5–7, 1969, shortly before requesting his transfer from Vietnam, Kerry was under the command of Captain Charles Plumly, USN, for an operation in which the Swifts transported mines and personnel near the Bay Hap River. The Swifts were assigned individual positions where they would wait should mine personnel be attacked or need assistance. Repeatedly, Kerry simply disappeared from position, "like a child with an attention problem," according to Captain Plumly. In Plumly's report to Admiral Hoffmann, he indicated to Hoffmann that he had a terrible problem with Kerry: Kerry simply would not obey orders. As a result, Hoffmann came to An Thoi and gave a talk to the officers there (not singling Kerry out), indicating that anyone who failed to obey orders in the future would be shipped to Saigon without further notice.

That Kerry stories abound is remarkable given his short cameo in Vietnam. Many recall Kerry blundering into living quarters in An Thoi with a live and dangerous Claymore mine and with B-40s that he had found. He acted like a tourist passing through, as if he intended to keep these items as souvenirs for later political campaigns. Like Lieutenant Keefer in *The Caine Mutiny*, the aspiring novelist played by Fred MacMurray in the 1954 movie, John Kerry kept busy with his private journal.

Kerry also often sported a home movie camera to record his exploits for later viewing. Swiftees report that Kerry would revisit ambush locations for reenacting combat scenes where he would portray the hero, catching it all on film. Kerry would take movies of himself walking around in combat gear, sometimes dressed as an infantryman walking resolutely through the terrain. He even filmed mock interviews of himself narrating his exploits. A joke circulated among Swiftees was that Kerry left Vietnam early not because he received three Purple Hearts, but because he had recorded enough film of himself to take home for his planned political campaigns.

Kerry's supporters point to an evaluation of Kerry by Commander George Elliott, who rated Kerry as "one of the few" best officers for his two months at An Thoi. In reality, Elliott gave essentially the same evaluation to every officer at An Thoi. Kerry was in the middle of the pack. Elliott felt that all the officers at An Thoi deserved superior ratings given the nature of the duty. Most important, Elliott did not know (as some of Kerry's peers had begun to learn) of Kerry's shell game of phony reports, fictitious victories, and concealed groundings. To the contrary, Kerry was ingratiating to superiors and, if judged solely by his own, often phony, written reports, a superb warrior proceeding from triumph to triumph. Commander Elliott notes that the tone and substance of Kerry's "reports" are captured quite succinctly in Churchill's quote, "I expect history to treat me kindly since I wrote it."

In his after-action reports, Kerry wove a story of often imagined enemy fire, nonexistent triumphs, and charges into intense fire against superior numbers of enemy. These accounts existed on paper, but almost never in the real world.

Captain Thomas Wright remembers that on multiboat operations Kerry would suddenly disappear without warning. He recalls that Kerry's boat had poor fire discipline and would open fire without prior clearance or apparent reason, sometimes opening fire even though the enemy had not fired at him. Because of these problems, Wright requested that Kerry no longer be assigned to operations under his command. Commander Elliott complied, and Wright no longer operated with Kerry.

Shortly before Kerry left Vietnam, Wright and others spoke to him at An Thoi. Kerry's three Purple Hearts would allow him to leave Vietnam, and they urged him to do so. Wright was not upset to see the "Boston Strangler" leave Vietnam. He believed that Kerry simply did not belong there. Kerry never formed the kind of human relationships with his fellow sailors that are essential to effective performance.

Purple Heart Number Two

Kerry claims to have been wounded on February 20, 1969, on the Dam Doi Canal, a canal running north from the Song Bo De River. In other reports, Kerry seems to place the location of the incident on the Cua Lon to the west. The operating report prepared by Kerry reflects "intense rocket and rifle fire." In his biography, Kerry describes "blood running down the deck":

> Just as they moved out onto the Cua Lon, at a junction known for unfriendliness in the past, kaboom! PCF 94 had taken a rocket-propelled grenade round off the port side, fired at them from the far left bank. Kerry felt a piece of hot shrapnel bore into his left leg. With blood running down the deck, the Swift managed to make an otherwise uneventful exit into the Gulf of Thailand, where they rendezvoused with a Coast Guard Cutter.[4]

The biography written by the *Boston Globe* reporters also acknowledges the wound, though the discussion of it is presented in a much less dramatic manner: "He was treated on an offshore ship and returned to duty hours later."[5]

The officer of the accompanying boat, Rocky Hildreth, states that John Kerry's operating report (which Hildreth did not see until 2004) is false, and that the intense rocket and rifle fire reported by Kerry never happened. It seems very unlikely that Kerry's boat could have experienced the heavy fire he reported without the accompanying boat hearing it. Hildreth also reports that there was no "blood on the deck," as Kerry claimed. Moreover, there was no damage to any boat from "the intense rifle and rocket fire" reported by Kerry. Van Odell, a sailor on PCF 93, recounts that when Kerry's crew came back that day, he heard them say that Kerry had faked a Purple Heart from his own M-79 wound. In addition, one of Kerry's crewmen, in a 2002 e-mail that he disowned after meeting with Kerry, questioned this Purple Heart and indicated that it was for a negligently self-inflicted M-79 grenade round like the one occurring at Cam Ranh Bay.

What is beyond question is that Kerry suffered at most a minor wound, losing no duty time. His account of "blood running down the deck" seems exaggerated, an awful lot of blood for a wound requiring what appears to have been minor treatment. If Kerry did suffer a minor wound from hostile fire on this occasion, this would have been the only time such a thing happened during his three months in Vietnam.

In his Dam Doi operating report from February 20, 1969, Kerry recommended "psy-ops" (psychological operations) along the Dam Doi—a recommendation he lauds as a great achievement in his 1970 interview in the *Harvard Crimson*: "One time Kerry was ordered to destroy a Viet Cong village but disobeyed orders and suggested that the Navy Command simply send in a Psychological Warfare team to befriend the villagers with food, hospital supplies, and better educational facilities."[6] Once again, Kerry promotes himself as an "antiwar warrior,"

Surprisingly, the Navy adopted a psy-ops recommendation. If the idea were indeed Kerry's, then it would have been the only such recommendation he made and the only one to be adopted. At any rate, the program was an unmitigated disaster. Many Swiftees, including John O'Neill, wondered who could have been so stupid as to recommend using our boats to travel slowly while playing psy-ops tapes over a loudspeaker, appealing in Vietnamese to the local population, in an area as hostile as the Dam Doi. Many Swiftees and Mobile Riverine Sailors died or were wounded on these missions following the "Boston Strangler's" recommendation.

One was Shelton White, a well-known film producer of underwater documentaries, who was wounded three times on the Dam Doi in a matter of minutes but who returned to fight again. White and many other sailors who signed the May 4, 2004, Swift Boat Veterans for the Truth letter opposing Kerry's presidential campaign did not realize even in 2004 that it was John Kerry who had recommended this ill-conceived psy-ops operation for which they had paid with their blood.

Ambush

A couple of days before his second Purple Heart, Kerry was also operating with Bob Hildreth, officer in charge of the accompanying boat. It was a day Hildreth would never forget. Kerry was the lead boat, with Hildreth behind. There was a small hole in a line of fishing stakes. Kerry's boat slipped through first. When Hildreth's boat started through, a mine went off, and then at least five rockets were fired at the boat. Standard doctrine and procedure when a boat was under such intense fire was for accompanying boats to stand and fight or return and provide fire support. According to Hildreth, Kerry simply fled, providing neither fire support nor even mortar support. Instead, Hildreth and his gallant crew were left alone to fight their way out of the ambush—which Hildreth has never forgotten: "I would never want Kerry behind me. I wouldn't want him in front of me either. And I sure wouldn't want him commanding our kids in Iraq and Afghanistan."

Typically, on Kerry's website, as well as in the operating report for that day, which Kerry wrote and Hildreth never saw, it is Kerry's boat—rather than Hildreth's—that encounters the five B-40s and the mine. Kerry's flight, leaving Hildreth's boat in serious jeopardy, vanishes from the account, and the event is a real triumph—at least on Kerry's website.

The Silver Star

For some thirty-five years, John Kerry has shaped his life around a single moment on February 28, 1969, for which he received the Silver Star. Unlike the lives of the Silver Star winners from Coastal Squadron One who signed the May 4, 2004, letter condemning John Kerry, or those of the sixty or so holders of one or more Purple Hearts in the same group, Kerry's life seems to be frozen at that moment. He has chosen to utilize his thirty-five-year-old Silver Star as the basis for every political campaign he has waged. In each campaign, a new participant in Kerry's medal stories is discovered, as was Jim Rassmann, the comrade "left behind" whom Kerry did fish out of the water but about whom he invented an exaggerated story during the 2004 presidential primary in Iowa. Each Kerry campaign ends with Kerry embracing his comrades while faulting his opponents for their less meritorious service.

Kerry's Star would never have been awarded had his actions been reviewed through normal channels. In his case, he was awarded the medal two days after the incident with no review. The medal was arranged to boost the morale of Coastal Division 11, but it was based on false and incomplete information provided by Kerry himself. Kerry did follow normal military conduct and displayed ordinary courage, but the incident was nothing out of the ordinary and to most Swift and Vietnam veterans, Kerry's actions would hardly justify any kind of unusual award. Moreover, to most Swiftees, Kerry's tactical judgment was very poor, reflecting a willingness to risk boat and crew for medals and personal glory—hardly the type of judgment we expect from a commander in chief.

The following is the Silver Star citation based on Kerry's account:

For conspicuous gallantry and intrepidity in action while serving with Coastal Division ELEVEN emerged in armed conflict with Viet Cong insurgents in An Xuyen Province, Republic of Vietnam, on 28 February 1969. Lieutenant (junior grade) KERRY was serving as Officer in Charge of Patrol Craft Fast 94 and Officer in Tactical Command of a three-boat mission. As the force approached the target area on the narrow Dong Cung River, all units came under intense automatic weapons and small arms fire from an entrenched enemy force less than fifty feet away. Unhesitatingly Lieutenant (junior grade) KERRY ordered his boat to attack as all units opened fire and beached directly in front of the enemy ambushers. This daring and courageous tactic surprised the enemy and succeeded in routing a score of enemy soldiers. The PCF gunners captured many enemy weapons in the battle that followed. On a request from U.S. Army advisors ashore, Lieutenant (junior grade) KERRY ordered PCFs 94 and 23 further up river to suppress enemy sniper fire. After proceeding approximately eight hundred yards, the boats were again taken under fire from a heavily foliated area and B-40 rocket exploded close aboard PCF 94; with utter disregard for his own safety and the enemy rockets, he again ordered a charge on the enemy, beached his boat only ten feet from the VC rocket position, and personally led a landing party ashore in pursuit of the enemy. Upon sweeping the area in an immediate search uncovered an enemy rest and supply area which was destroyed. The extraordinary daring and personal courage of Lieutenant (junior grade) KERRY in attacking a numerically superior force in the face of intense fire were responsible for the highly successful mission. His actions were in keeping with the highest traditions of the United States Naval Service.[7]

What actually occurred was quite different. According to Kerry's crewman Michael Medeiros, Kerry had an agreement with him to turn the boat in and onto the beach if fired upon. Each of the three boats involved in the operation was involved in the agreement. Larry Lee, a crewman and gunner, recalls the agreement as Medeiros recounts it and further recalls a prior discussion of probable medals for those participating. Bronze Stars for selected landers were contemplated and Navy commendation for others. Some crewmen dispute this, but none deny that the landing had been calculated the night before.

According to Doug Reese, a pro-Kerry Army veteran, and many others, what happened that day differs from the retelling in the citation. Far from being alone, the boats were loaded with many soldiers commanded by Reese and two other advisors. When fired at, Reese's boat—not Kerry's—was the first to beach in the ambush zone. Then Reese and other troops and advisors (not Kerry) disembarked, killing a number of Viet Cong and capturing a number of weapons. None of the participants from Reese's boat received any Silver Stars. Indeed, most, if not all, of the non-PCF troops received no medals for this action. Doug Reese, who advised the South Vietnamese who were the first group ashore and who killed most of the Viet Cong, received a well-deserved Army Commendation Medal—a much lower medal than the Silver Star. After the first boat beached, Kerry's boat moved slightly downstream and was struck by a rocket-propelled grenade in its aft cabin.

A young Viet Cong in a loincloth popped out of a hole, clutching a grenade launcher which may or may not have been loaded, depending on whose account one credits.[8] Tom Belodeau, a forward gunner, shot the Viet Cong with an M-60 machine gun in the leg as he fled.[9] At about this time, with the boat beached, the Viet Cong who had been wounded by Belodeau fled. Kerry and Medeiros (who had many troops in their boat) took off, perhaps with others, following the young Viet Cong as he fled, and shot him in the back, behind a lean-to. While Kerry's actions in shooting a wounded, fleeing teenage foe were criticized in various 1996 *Boston Globe* articles and by some Swiftees, Kerry was defended in a 1996 press conference by Admiral Zumwalt, Captain Adrian Lonsdale, and Captain Elliott—a critical event in Kerry's bid for reelection to the Senate that year. Ironically, each of the officers who were requested by Kerry to defend him in 1996 also signed the May 4, 2004, letter, condemning Kerry for his own many misrepresentations of his record and the record of others.[10]

Whether Kerry's dispatching of a fleeing, wounded, armed, or unarmed teenage enemy was in accordance with the customs of war, it is very clear that many Vietnam veterans and most Swiftees do not consider this action to be the stuff of which medals of any kind are awarded; nor would it even be a good story if told in the cold details of reality. There is no indication that Kerry ever reported that the Viet Cong was wounded and fleeing when dispatched. Likewise, the citation simply ignores the presence of the soldiers and advisors who actually "captured the many enemy weapons" and routed the Viet Cong. Further, the citation ignores the preplanned nature of the tactic and the fact that Kerry's boat did not beach first. Finally, the citation statement that Kerry attacked "a numerically superior force in the face of intense fire" is simply false. There was little or no fire after Kerry followed the plan (and the earlier move of the first boat toward the beach). The lone, wounded, fleeing young Viet Cong in a loincloth was hardly a force superior to the heavily armed Swift boat and its crew and the soldiers carried aboard.[11]

The actual facts disclosed in 1996 and thereafter by Kerry's crewmen and others like Reese, who are among the small minority of pro-Kerry Swiftees and Vietnam veterans, are completely at odds with the purported "facts" discussed in the citation. Admiral Roy Hoffmann, who sent a Bravo Zulu (meaning "good work") to Kerry upon learning of the incident, was very surprised to discover in 2004 what had actually occurred. Hoffmann had been told that Kerry had spontaneously beached next to the bunker and almost single-handedly routed a bunkered force of Viet Cong. He was shocked to find out that Kerry had beached his boat second in a preplanned operation, and that he had killed a single, wounded teenage foe as he fled.

The planned nature of the action also calls Kerry's judgment into doubt. The effect of beaching a boat is to risk the loss of all aboard, as well as the boat itself, because of the Claymore mines often found in front of bunkered positions. Moreover, the heavy weapons of the boat, double .50-caliber machine guns and an M-60, are unusable if friendly soldiers are in front of them. In effect, a single sailor with no radio or means of communications, armed with a single M-16, is substituted for the vast firepower of the boat. Finally, once the boat is beached, speed and maneuverability are obviously gone. The boat is frozen, shorn of its command function, in a single spot.

From a military viewpoint, the tactic displays stupidity, not courage—a point that has made it so hard for Vietnam Navy veterans (sometimes called "brown-water sailors" after the color of the water in the muddy Vietnamese delta), from vice admirals to seamen, to believe it. Brown-water officers and Swiftees willing to forgive stupidity when the action is a spontaneous charge against an enemy bunker undertaken by a foolhardy young officer, were appalled to learn recently that the action was actually preplanned by Kerry, who then wildly exaggerated the facts in his citation: from the "PCF gunners" capturing many weapons to his assault under "intense fire" into a bunker manned by "a numerically superior force." The only explanation for what Kerry did is the same justification that characterizes his entire short Vietnam adventure: the pursuit of medals and ribbons. Kerry's self-serving exaggeration of the action magnified the danger he faced and the supposed valor he displayed, and minimized or showed no appreciation for the actual nature of the risk or the contribution of the others involved.[12]

Commander George Elliott, who wrote up the initial draft of Kerry's Silver Star citation, confirms that neither he nor anyone else in the Silver Star process that he knows realized before 1996 that Kerry was facing a single, wounded young Viet Cong fleeing in a loincloth. While Commander Elliott and many other Swiftees believe that Kerry committed no crime in killing the fleeing, wounded enemy (with a loaded or empty launcher), others feel differently. Commander Elliott indicates that a Silver Star recommendation would not have been made by him had he been aware of the actual facts. A more appropriate award for Kerry, if any, would have been the much lower Army Commendation Medal given to Doug Reese.

Swiftees have no answer (beyond that we simply did not know the actual facts) to the numerous Marine and Army veterans of Hue City, Khe Sanh, and other battles who have sent e-mails asking how Kerry could have possibly received a Silver Star for this limited achievement.

The various other Silver Stars won by many of the signers of the May 4, 2004, statement opposing Kerry are stories of extraordinary heroism—stories that the nation will never hear. They are truly heroic acts: genuine charges into unknown hostile territory under intense fire, rescues of half-sunken boats with dead or wounded crews under horrible fire, and placing boats between the enemy and wounded, disabled, and dying to intercept the bombardment. These stories will never be used for self-advantage by the real heroes of our unit. In several cases, these tales are known only to themselves and God, unknown even to their children and families.

The Third Purple Heart and the Bronze Star

On March 13, 1969, John Kerry was involved in his final "combat" in Vietnam. The public has seen it. The incident has been the subject of more than $50 million in paid political advertising and was featured in the 2004 Democratic presidential primary in Iowa, where Kerry met in tearful reunion with Jim Rassmann, the Special Forces lieutenant "rescued from the water" by Kerry.

The following is Kerry's account of the final episode of his Vietnam cameo: A mine went off alongside Kerry's boat. Lieutenant Rassmann was blown into the water. Kerry was terribly wounded from the underwater mine. Kerry turned back into the fire zone and, bleeding heavily from his arm and side, reached into the water and pulled Rassmann to safety with enemy fire all around. Kerry then towed a sinking boat out of the action.

There is only one problem with this scenario: The above recounting is another gross exaggeration of what actually happened and, in several ways, is a total fraud perpetrated upon the Navy and the nation. Kerry's conduct on March 13, 1969, was more worthy of disciplinary action than any sort of medal. The action certainly does not establish Kerry's credentials for becoming the president of the United States.

Kerry's March 13, 1969, "Medals"

According to the records, Kerry claimed in the casualty report he prepared on March 13, 1969, that he was wounded as a result of a mine explosion. Within a short period, he presented his request to go home on the basis of his three Purple Hearts. By March 17, 1969, Kerry's short combat career in Vietnam was over.

Regarding the action on March 13, 1969, Kerry's medals were once again a complete fraud. Notwithstanding the fake submission for his Bronze Star, Kerry was never wounded or bleeding from his arm. All reports, including the medical reports, make clear that he suffered a minor bruise on his arm and minor shrapnel wounds on his buttocks. The minor bruise on his arm would never have justified a Purple Heart and is not mentioned in the citation.

This leaves only Kerry's rear-end wound. This wound, like the Cam Ranh Bay wound, was of the minor tweezer-and-Band-Aid variety. How did Kerry receive a shrapnel wound in his buttocks from the explosion of an underwater mine, as his report suggests? Many participants in the incident state that neither weapons fire nor a mine explosion occurred near Kerry during the incident.

Larry Thurlow, an experienced, genuine hero and PCF veteran, commanded the boat behind Kerry on March 13, 1969. Thurlow was on the shore with Kerry and a group of Nung soldiers (mercenaries working with the South Vietnamese) that morning of March 13, 1969. Thurlow recalls that Kerry had that morning wounded himself in the buttocks with a grenade that he set off too close to a stock of rice he was trying to destroy. The incident is all too reminiscent of the M-79 grenade Kerry exploded too close to some rocks on shore, causing the wound at Cam Ranh Bay that resulted in his first Purple Heart. As the *Boston Globe* biographers note:

> At one point, Kerry and Rassmann threw grenades into a huge rice cache that had been captured from the Vietcong and was thus slated for destruction. After tossing the grenades, the two dove for cover. Rassmann escaped the ensuing explosion of rice, but Kerry was not as lucky—thousands of grains stuck to him. The result was hilarious, and the two men formed a bond.[13]

Very probably, the incident Rassmann describes that resulted in Kerry's self-inflicted wound is the very wound that Kerry used to claim his final Purple Heart. Indeed, Kerry's report for that day mentions the rice he destroyed. He dishonestly transferred the time and cause of the injury to coincide with the PCF action later in the day and claimed that the cause of the injury was the mine exploding during the action.

By March 1969, most of Kerry's peers at An Thoi were aware of his reputation as an unscrupulous self-promoter with an insatiable appetite for medals. But no one actually understood what Kerry pulled off. When Thurlow finally realized that the PCF 3 incident was the same incident described by the Kerry advertisement and in *Tour of Duty*, Thurlow instantly knew that Kerry had used the PCF 3 mine explosion and tragedy for its crew as his ticket home. Thurlow was astounded by the metamorphosis that had taken place in the explanation of Kerry's wound: from Kerry's own grenade as a cause, which Thurlow knew about; to a grenade error by friendly forces in the absence of hostile fire (Kerry's secret journal and *Tour of Duty*); and then finally to the mine explosion (Kerry's report and Purple Heart citation).

Unfortunately for Kerry, he ended up telling the truth by mistake. On page 313 of *Tour of Duty* and evidently in his secret journal writ-

Bill Lupetti

Photo of John Kerry and Vietnam's former General Secretary of the Communist Party Do Muoi. The photo is part of an exhibit honoring heroes who had helped the Vietnamese Communists win the war against the United States. The photo is displayed in the War Remnants Museum in Ho Chi Minh City.

Bill Lupetti

A sign on the entrance of the War Remnants Museum. The museum, originally called the "War Crimes Museum," was established in 1975 to focus on alleged American war crimes.

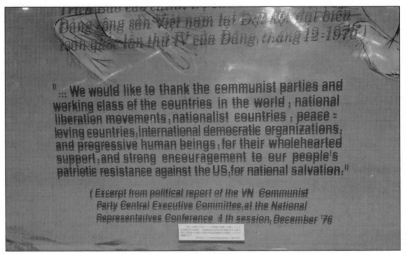

Bill Lupetti

A wall plaque that describes the theme of the hall that displays Kerry's photo: "We would like to thank the communist parties and working class of the countries of the world, national liberation movements, nationalist countries, peace-loving countries, international democratic organizations, and progressive human beings for their wholehearted support, and strong encouragement to our people's patriotic resistance against the U.S. for national salvation."

Bill Lupetti

The exhibit that dislays Kerry's photo also shows this photo of David Miller, who publicly burned his draft notice in 1965. Miller's action inspired similar protests in the antiwar movement.

A photo of Jane Fonda with Madame Binh is displayed in a separate Women's Museum in Ho Chi Minh City.

Bill Lupetti

The 1971 O'Neill-Kerry debate on the *Dick Cavett Show*. O'Neill challenges Kerry to provide specific instances of atrocities and war crimes that occurred in their Swift Boat unit, Coastal Division 11. Kerry failed to provide any specific examples.

John O'Neill

John O'Neill and John Kerry appeared in several forums in 1971.

Bettmann/Corbis

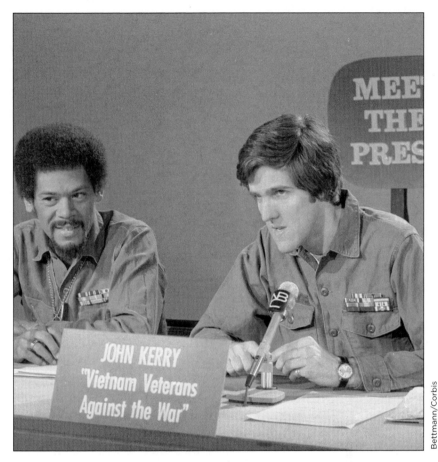

Bettmann/Corbis

John Kerry and Al Hubbard on *Meet the Press* in April 18, 1971. Kerry was asked if he himself had committed any war crimes or atrocities in Vietnam. Kerry answered that he had (partial transcript on page 153).

Leif Skoogfors/Corbis

Kerry and Jane Fonda at a 1970 antiwar rally in Valley Forge, Pennsylvania. (Kerry is directly above Jane Fonda's head.)

WinterSoldier.com

This photograph of 20 Swift Boat officers, including Kerry, runs in Kerry's campaign commercials. Eleven officers have called upon Kerry to stop using their image. Of the remaining eight, two are deceased, four do not wish to be involved and one is not a supporter of Kerry, but did not have an opportunity to sign the letter requesting that the image not be used. Only one of the nineteen is believed to support Kerry.

The same photo identifies the name of each officer and whether he supports Kerry's presidential campaign.

The same photo showing John Kerry and the only sailor who supports Kerry's bid for president.

John O'Neill with his crew of PCF 94 in Vietnam.

John O'Neill

ten on or about March 13, 1969, which is quoted in the book, Kerry relates his injury from the rice stock explosion, although he tries to place the time and context of the incident later in the day and tries to claim that it resulted from friendly forces (the Nungs) but at a time in which there was no hostile fire:

> The Nung blew up some huge bins of rice they had found, as it was assumed, as always, that these were the local stockpiles earmarked to feed the hungry VC moving through the Delta smuggling weapons. "I got a piece of small grenade in my ass from one of the rice-bin explosions and then we started to move back to the boats, firing to our rear as we went."[14]

Unless one believes in the amazing coincidence that Kerry got two wounds in the same place on the same day and from the same type of incident, then Kerry's wound of March 13, 1969, was not the result of hostile fire at all but, once again, simply a self-inflicted minor wound about which he lied to get a Purple Heart. Whatever the facts of the March 13 incident, it seems incontrovertible that: (1) Kerry lied in the Bronze Star citation about having any arm wound other than a minor bruise; and (2) Kerry fraudulently secured a Purple Heart by falsely attributing his self-inflicted "piece of small grenade in my ass" to the mine explosion hitting PCF 3 or to any other hostile action.

What Actually Happened

In addition to fabricating wounds from hostile fire to gain his third Purple Heart, a Bronze Star, and a quick trip home, Kerry falsely described the incident in his 1969 operating report, in his campaign biography, in his advertising, and even on his 2004 campaign website. On March 13, 1969, Jack Chenoweth commanded the boat in front of

Kerry, and his gunner, Van Odell, had a clear view of the entire incident. Dick Pease commanded PCF 3, which was blown up by the mine that day. None of these Swiftees recognized the incident as described by Kerry in his report, by Douglas Brinkley in *Tour of Duty*, or on Kerry's website. They were furious when they realized Kerry's fraudulent account.

In reality, Kerry's boat was on the right side of the river when a mine went off on the opposite side, under PCF 3. The boat's crewmen were thrown into the water. The officers of PCF 3 were injured by the explosion and suffered concussions. A Viet Cong sympathizer in an adjoining bunker had touched off the mine. Besides the mine exploding under PCF 3, there was no other hostile fire and there were no other mines, according to Chenoweth, Odell, Pease, and Thurlow. The boats had begun firing after the mine exploded, but they ceased after a short time because of the lack of hostile fire.

Despite the absence of hostile fire, Kerry fled the scene. The remaining PCFs, in accord with standard doctrine, stood to defend the disabled PCF 3 and its crewmen in the water. Kerry disappeared several hundred yards away, returning only when it was clear that there was no return fire.

Chenoweth (who received no medal) picked up the PCF 3 crewmen thrown into the water. As a result of the explosion, PCF 3's engines were knocked out on one side and frozen on 500 RPM on the other side. The boat weaved dangerously, hitting sandbars, with a dazed or unconscious crew aboard. Thurlow sought a secure hold on his boat so he could jump across and board PCF 3. However, he was thrown into the water as his first attempt to board PCF 3 failed and the boat hit the sandbars. Later, Thurlow brought PCF 3 to a stop, and the boat slowly began to sink.

During the incident, Jim Rassmann had fallen or had been knocked off either Kerry's boat or PCF 35. When he was spotted in the water,

Chenoweth's boat, with the PCF 3 crew aboard, went to pick him up. Kerry's boat, returning to the scene after its flight, reached him about twenty yards before Chenoweth.

Kerry did the decent thing by going a short distance to pick up Rassmann, justifiably earning Rassmann's gratitude. The claim that Kerry "returned" to a hostile fire zone is a lie according to Chenoweth, Thurlow, and many others. Meanwhile, the serious work of saving PCF 3 continued.

Kerry's false after-action report, prepared to justify his medals, reports "5,000 meters"—about two and a half miles—of heavy fire, about the same distance as a large Civil War battlefield. Not a shot of this fire was heard by Chenoweth, Thurlow, Odell, or Pease. Kerry's false after-action report ignores Chenoweth's heroic action in rescuing the PCF 3 survivors and Thurlow's action in saving PCF 3, while highlighting his own routine pickup of Rassmann and PCF 94's minor role in saving PCF 3.

When Chenoweth's boat left a second time to deliver the wounded PCF 3 crewmen to a Coast Guard cutter offshore, Kerry jumped into the boat, leaving the few remaining officers and men the job of saving PCF 3, which was then in terrible condition, sinking just outside the river. Kerry's eagerness to secure his third and final Purple Heart evidently outweighed any feelings he may have had of loyalty, duty, or honor with regard to his fellow sailors. Thurlow and the brave sailors who saved PCF 3 and towed it out did not seek Purple Hearts for their "minor contusions." Indeed, several of the PCF 3 sailors did not seek or receive Purple Hearts. Chenoweth, Odell, and their boatmates who fished out and saved the sailors of PCF 3 likewise had no thought of seeking medals but only of rescuing their comrades and saving PCF 3. Kerry, however, portrays himself towing the disabled PCF 3 to safety after saving it. Another lie: The damage control on PCF 3 was done by Thurlow. While Kerry's boat, PCF 94, participated in towing PCF 3, Kerry was no longer on it for most of the trip (he was safely on the Coast Guard cutter), and Thurlow and Chenoweth are certain that Kerry played no role in saving PCF 3 or its crew.

When Chenoweth and Thurlow (as well as several other Swiftees who were there on March 13, 1969) first saw the Kerry ads, they believed the event that Kerry had described in his campaign biography and that was portrayed in his campaign television ads (as well as in the medal citations) had to be different events involving different people. What they had experienced on March 13, 1969, was so unlike the incident Kerry described that they could not imagine that he was describing the same event. They were horrified when they finally realized Kerry had received medals for the incident they remembered.

Rassmann appeared for a spontaneous embrace of Kerry at a campaign event in Iowa. He was understandably grateful to Kerry for fishing him out of the river, and he was evidently happy to participate in the "no man left behind" version of the story being told by Kerry in his "war hero" mode. As with most Kerry campaigns, Iowa ended with Kerry, the Vietnam hero. Still, the other Swiftees who learned of Kerry's fraudulent citations and ads felt betrayed. William Franke, writes,

> You've just got to make them understand. We went out to operate and survive. We had no time to deal with the crap of John Kerry. We weren't thinking of self-promotion like him. Just survival and doing the job. We didn't want him around and we were happy he was gone.[15]

Tom Wright, another PCF commander at An Thoi, discussed John Kerry with several other Swiftees on base right after the March 13 incident. They were aware of the three Purple Heart rule that sounded like "three strikes and you're out." John Kerry could be sent home. So Wright approached Kerry one night and proposed to him that several fellow Swiftees on the base felt that it might be best for everybody if Kerry simply left. The next thing Wright knew, Kerry was gone, the exact result Wright hoped to achieve.

Coming Home

Kerry followed up the March Purple Heart with a request to head home, the only Swiftee in the history of Coastal Division 11 to do so before the end of a tour, except of course, those who suffered a serious wound.[16] Kerry arrived home in New York, completing his "one-year tour" in the record time of four months. According to his biography, when he got off the airplane at Kennedy Airport in New York to meet his fiancée, Julia Thorne, Kerry was supposedly so "bandaged" that "some of it was sticking out."[17] Whether this was just another example of Kerry political theater is not clear. It is certain that Kerry had only a minor bruise on his arm and a minor self-inflicted wound on the buttocks from some two weeks earlier. It is unclear how either of these wounds could have accounted for bandages "sticking out" from his clothing.

In his 1971 debate on the *Dick Cavett Show* with John O'Neill, Kerry made it seem as if his decision process to leave Vietnam had been tortured:

> The fact of the matter remains that after I received my third wound, I was told that I could return to the United States. *I deliberated for about two weeks* because there was a difficult decision in whether or not you leave your friends because you have an opportunity to go, but I finally made the decision to go

back and did leave of my own volition because I felt I could do more against the war back here....When I got back here...I wrote a letter through him [an admiral] requesting that I be released from the Navy early *because of my opposition.*[18]

This "deliberation" was once again a complete lie. Kerry was "wounded" on March 13, 1969, on the Bay Hap River, but by March 17, 1969, at 7:42 a.m., his request for reassignment to the United States (having been typed up far away in An Thoi and signed by the commander there) was at the Navy Department in Washington. His subsequent request to leave the Navy late in 1969 mentions nothing about his "opposition to the war," but only his ambition to run for Congress.[19]

The real Kerry "homecoming" that most Swiftees will never forget occurred at St. Albans Naval Hospital in early April 1969, where Tedd Peck, the commander of PCF 94, lay recovering from terrible wounds that he suffered on January 29, 1969.[20] Peck was horrified when he learned that PCF 94 and his crew had been turned over to Kerry after Peck had been wounded. He thought, "How could the Navy do this to me after all I've suffered?"

Still in pain and suffering from his wounds, Peck was stunned to see a well-groomed John Kerry pop into his room, complete with dress whites and attaché cord. "Kerry, you son of a bitch," Peck said, "what the hell are you doing here? You were only there a couple of months."

Kerry replied (lying about his own request to come home), "Tedd, the Navy decided it was time for me to come home." Kerry explained that he was visiting the wounded as an admiral's aide.

Within a short time, Kerry sought to recruit Peck for the Vietnam Veterans Against the War (VVAW), which Kerry described as a group he had organized. Peck, dumbfounded, asked Kerry, "John, how can you do this? All of our guys are still over there, in Vietnam?"

Kerry had no answer.

We have never been given any more of a real answer from John Kerry than the one Tedd Peck received while lying in his hospital bed.

PART TWO

ANTIWAR PROTESTER

SIX

A TESTIMONY OF LIES

"Lt. Kerry returned home from the war to make some outrageous statements and allegations. Numerous criminal acts in violations of the law of war were cited by Kerry, disparaging those who had fought with honor in that conflict."

LT. COL. JAMES ZUMWALT, USMC (RETIRED)

Swift Boat Veterans for Truth Press Conference
Washington, D.C., May 4, 2004

The Fulbright Committee

Inside the committee room the television cameras were ready, lights glaring. A group of scraggly young men in a ragtag mixture of military uniforms accompanied by hippie-looking young women filled the front seats behind the witness chair. John Kerry's supporters from the Vietnam Veterans Against the War (VVAW) were here to applaud their leader.

Kerry's testimony to the Fulbright Committee was a carefully orchestrated piece of political theater. Fulbright wanted a presentable, young Kennedy-esque face to put on the antiwar effort, and Kerry wanted a national forum from which to launch his climb to political celebrity. Ted Kennedy helped arrange Kerry's testimony with Senator Fulbright at a private fundraising event held at the home of Democratic senator Philip A. Hart of Michigan.

Kerry was late. The anticipation in the room was building as the audience looked around to see if the man of the moment was anywhere in the hall. Then Kerry, slightly out of breath, burst into the hall from the back door. He charged into the room and strode directly forward to Senator Fulbright. He extended his hand, his long jaw set firmly forward. There was a sense of adrenaline about him. He worked the front of the room, approaching each senator and extending his hand, speaking softly to them as if he had known them for years, commanding the attention of all in the room, the cameras already recording the action.

As Kerry settled into the witness chair, he folded his hands in front of him, his military fatigues open at the collar to reveal his T-shirt beneath, the bands of ribbons above his left pocket—there both to call attention to his service decorations and to signal to those in the know the insult communicated by the inappropriate wearing of service bars in anything but dress uniform. His mop of hair was stylishly swept across his forehead, and his mouth was firmly closed in a thin, determined line. Kerry was ready for his cue; his studied testimony, carefully practiced, was ready for delivery. He patiently waited his moment to burst onto the national scene.

Chairman Fulbright brought the committee to order:

The committee is continuing this morning its hearings on proposals relating to the ending of the war in Southeast Asia. This morning the committee will hear testimony from Mr. John Kerry and, if he has any associates, we will be glad to hear from them. These are men who have fought in this unfortunate war in Vietnam. I believe they deserve to be heard and listened to by the Congress and by the officials in the executive branch and by the public generally. You have a perspective that those in the Government who make our Nation's policy do not always have and I am sure that your testimony today will be helpful to the committee in its consideration of the proposals before us.

Senator Fulbright left no doubt that the committee had a political agenda and was decidedly antiwar. What were John Kerry's credentials? He was a veteran who had been in Vietnam, and his perspective opposing the war was one that Senator Fulbright wanted heard. Next, Senator Fulbright apologized that the Supreme Court had issued an injunction forbidding the VVAW protesters from camping out on the National Mall.

I would like to add simply on my own account that I regret very much the action of the Supreme Court in denying the veterans the right to use the Mall. [Applause]

Senator Fulbright left no doubt where he stood on the issue of the Vietnam War:

I have joined with some of my colleagues, specifically Senator Hart, in an effort to try to change the attitude of our Government toward your efforts in bringing to this committee and to the country your views about the war.

I personally don't know of any group that would have both a greater justification for doing it and also a more accurate view of the effect of the war. As you know, there has grown up in this town a feeling that it is extremely difficult to get accurate information about the war and I don't know a better source than you and your associates. So we are very pleased to have you and your associates, Mr. Kerry.

John O'Neill, a Navy veteran who had also served in Vietnam in Coastal Division 11, had written to the committee asking for an opportunity to give his testimony. The committee's written response indicated that the schedule was very full and that there would be no time available. John O'Neill supported the war in Vietnam.

John Kerry began his statement:

> Thank you very much, Senator Fulbright, Senator Javits, Senator Symington, Senator Pell. I would like to say for the record, and also for the men behind me who are also wearing the uniforms and their medals, that my sitting here is really symbolic. I am not here as John Kerry. I am here as one member of the group of one thousand, which is a small representation of a very much larger group of veterans in this country, and were it possible for all of them to sit at this table they would be here and have the same kind of testimony.
>
> I would simply like to speak in very general terms. I apologize if my statement is general because I received notification yesterday you would hear me and I am afraid because of the injunction I was up most of the night and haven't had a great deal of time to prepare.

What about the cocktail party at Senator Hart's home days before? Once Kerry learned that he would have the chance to give testimony before the committee, he recruited the assistance of Adam Walinsky, a speechwriter noted for his work with Robert Kennedy. Walinsky drafted the speech and coached Kerry on its delivery. The only image

Kerry wanted us to see was a myth: a young man with a burning passion for the truth, the leader forced to sleep on the ground, the man answering his country's call to be where he was urgently needed, before a committee of the United States Senate where the senators and America were urgently waiting for his firsthand criticism of the war. He proceeded to level his charges:

> I would like to talk, representing all those veterans, and say that several months ago in Detroit, we had an investigation at which over 150 honorably discharged and many very highly decorated veterans testified to war crimes committed in Southeast Asia, not isolated incidents but crimes committed on a day-to-day basis with the full awareness of officers at all levels of command.
>
> It is impossible to describe to you exactly what did happen in Detroit, the emotions in the room, the feelings of the men who were reliving their experiences in Vietnam, but they did. They relived the absolute horror of what this country, in a sense, made them do.
>
> They told the stories at times they had personally raped, cut off ears, cut off heads, taped wires from portable telephones to human genitals and turned up the power, cut off limbs, blown up bodies, randomly shot at civilians, razed villages in a fashion reminiscent of Ghengis Khan, shot cattle and dogs for fun, poisoned food stocks, and generally ravaged the countryside of South Vietnam in addition to the normal ravage of war, and the normal and very particular ravaging which is done by the applied bombing power of this country.

Kerry's testimony was shocking and graphic, a slap in the face to the military personnel who were at that very moment fighting and dying in Vietnam. Yet he produced no documentation. Where were the specific incidents? Where were the affidavits? Kerry presented only unsubstantiated charges. As we will see, not only was the testimony given in Detroit at what was called the Winter Soldier Investigation unsubstantiated, but much of it was fraudulent. Kerry had the attention of the Senate; why didn't he present proof? Possibly because he had none. The core of Kerry's argument was that fighting in Vietnam was pointless:

In our opinion, and from our experience, there is nothing in South Vietnam, nothing which could happen that realistically threatens the United States of America. And to attempt to justify the loss of one American life in Vietnam, Cambodia, or Laos by linking such loss to the preservation of freedom... is to us the height of criminal hypocrisy, and it is that kind of hypocrisy which we feel has torn this country apart.

The contrast with John F. Kennedy's Inaugural Address was clear: "Let every nation know, whether it wishes us well or ill, that we shall pay any price, bear any burden, meet any hardship, support any friend, oppose any foe, in order to assure the survival and the success of liberty." Kerry characterized the Vietnam War not as an effort to save the country from Communism but as a civil war or, possibly, a war waged in an effort to free the nation from colonialism, a war in which our allies, the South Vietnamese, were not defenders of freedom. He continued:

We found that not only was it a civil war, an effort by a people who had for years been seeking their liberation from any colonial influence whatsoever, but also we found that the Vietnamese whom we had enthusiastically molded after our own image were hard put to take up the fight against the threat we were supposedly saving them from.

We found that most people didn't even know the difference between communism and democracy. They only wanted to work in rice paddies without helicopters strafing them and bombs with napalm burning their villages and tearing their country apart. They wanted everything to do with the war, particularly with this foreign presence of the United States of America, to leave them alone in peace, and they practiced the art of survival by siding with whichever military force was present at a particular time, be it Vietcong, North Vietnamese, or American.

Kerry drew a moral equivalence between the military force that we were exerting to establish liberty and the violence used by the Viet Cong and North Vietnamese to establish Communism. He suggested that we might be just another colonial force in that part of the world, ourselves morally wrong.

We found also that all too often American men were dying in those rice paddies for want of support from their allies. We saw firsthand how money from American taxes was used for a corrupt dictatorial regime. We saw that many people in this country had a one-sided idea of who was kept free by our flag, as blacks provided the highest percentage of casualties. We saw Vietnam ravaged equally by American bombs as well as by search and destroy missions, as well as by Vietcong terrorism, and yet we listened while this country tried to blame all of the havoc on the Vietcong.

Kerry then proceeded to a carefully crafted section, a string of "we rationalized…we learned…we watched" statements indicting American warfare in Vietnam, emphasizing his view that American racism was responsible for military abuses. This was very polished rhetoric for a speech that supposedly was thrown together overnight. Why didn't Kerry just tell the panel the truth—that he had been working on the speech for some time and that he had professional help putting it together?

We rationalized destroying villages in order to save them. We saw America lose her sense of morality as she accepted very coolly a My Lai and refused to give up the image of American soldiers who hand out chocolate bars and chewing gum.

We learned the meaning of free-fire zones, shooting anything that moves, and we watched while America placed a cheapness on the lives of Orientals.

We watched the U.S. falsification of body counts, in fact the glorification of body counts. We listened while month after month we were told the back of the enemy was about to break.

We fought using weapons against "oriental human beings," with quotation marks around that. We fought using weapons against those people which I do not believe this country would dream of using were we fighting in the European theater, or let us say a non-third-world people theater.

Adam Walinsky later bragged that Kerry, the 1966 Yale class orator, was "pretty darn good" with words all by himself, but that the parts of Kerry's speech that showed up on television were the product of his hand, not Kerry's.[1] Yet Kerry was well aware that his main goal was to create an impression before the cameras. The entire protest week in Washington, D.C., had been for Kerry an exercise in high political theater. While his VVAW comrades had slept on the Mall, camping out as part of their protest, Kerry and his girlfriend had slipped away to sleep in comfort, welcomed into the fancy George-town homes of politically sympathetic family friends.

Kerry built to his conclusion with a question that has become the most repeated part of the speech: "How do you ask a man to be the last man to die for a mistake?"

The argument presented by Kerry was based on viewing the Viet-nam War as a mistake. If one saw the war as an important step in the Cold War determination to stop the spread of Communism (a view held by President Johnson and President Nixon), then asking men to die was consistent with President Kennedy's pledge that we would pay such a precious price to preserve liberty in a free world.

Perhaps this is the question that needs to be asked by the Ameri-can people and answered by John Kerry: Who was the last American POW to die languishing in a North Vietnamese prison, forced to lis-ten to the recorded voice of John Kerry disgracing his service by dis-honest testimony before the Senate?

Paul Galanti, a Navy pilot who was shot down over Vietnam in June 1966 and then spent seven years in Communist captivity as a POW, remembers Kerry's antiwar rhetoric all too well. Galanti told the *Los Angeles Times* in February 2004 that during torture sessions his North Vietnamese captors had cited antiwar speeches as "an example of why we should cross over to [their] side." As far as Galanti was concerned, "Kerry broke a covenant among servicemen never to make public criticisms that might jeopardize those still in battle or in the hands of the enemy." Galanti's criticism of Kerry was particu-larly biting: "John Kerry was a traitor to the men he served with." Now retired and in his sixties, Galanti refuses to abandon his anger at Kerry. "I don't plan to set it aside. I don't know anyone who does," he was quoted as saying. "The Vietnam memorial has thousands of additional names due to John Kerry and others like him."[2]

Still, Senator Kerry refuses to consider that his testimony caused more deaths and prolonged the war in Vietnam by undermining support at home and contributing directly to a Vietnamese Communist victory.

The Winter Soldier Investigation

Kerry's testimony to the Fulbright Committee referenced the testimony given at the Winter Soldier Investigation as the basis of his conclusion that war crimes and atrocities were being committed in Vietnam. This "investigation" was supposedly his entire foundation for the charges he had made. What was the Winter Soldier Investigation? How credible was the testimony given there?

The phrase "winter soldier" was derived from pamphleteer Thomas Paine, whose *American Crisis* on December 23, 1776, contained the now-famous words referring to George Washington's troops, who braved the depths of snow and cold at Valley Forge through the bitter winter of 1777–78: "These are the times that try men's souls. The summer soldier and the sunshine patriot will, in the crisis, shrink from the services of their country; but he that stands it now deserves the love and thanks of men and women." The VVAW adopted the term "winter soldier" to symbolize their professed toughness, their dedication to expose what they considered the criminal behavior at the core of a war they say was immoral, the realities only a real soldier—a "winter soldier"—would have the courage to profess.

The idea for the investigation was relatively simple. A VVAW panel would call veterans as witnesses and take testimony from them about atrocities they had witnessed or committed in Vietnam. In truth, this was not an investigation at all. There were no thorough background checks of those testifying, no independent corroboration of the testimony given, not even any sworn statements to hold those testifying to some sort of legal standard of veracity.

Why? There was a deeper political level to the agenda. More important than establishing beyond doubt that the testifying veterans had actually witnessed war crimes in Vietnam or had committed atrocities themselves, the Winter Soldier Investigation aimed to shock the public. Sensationalism, not honesty, was the operative standard.

The critical political goal was to demonstrate that the atrocities described were a direct result of U.S. military policy, not random acts of meaningless or unauthorized cruelty. This was consistent with the argument advanced by Kerry before the Fulbright Committee. The contention was that American military policy in Vietnam necessarily resulted in the commission of war crimes, that the atrocities committed were commonplace occurrences, and that military commanders condoned these war crimes as a necessary result of the orders they had issued. Otherwise, all that would be established was that the men testifying might well be just criminals. The VVAW had no intention of pointing the finger at the soldiers themselves; the goal was to indict the United States military, all the way up the chain of command to the Joint Chiefs of Staff and, ultimately, to President Nixon. The government of the United States was the target. The soldiers in the field were only the pawns used to get there.

Noted extremists were involved in organizing the Winter Soldier Investigation. Jane Fonda was a key financial supporter and the honorary national coordinator of the event. This was Fonda's Mao period, complete with Viet Cong flags, red star costumes, and frequently photographed expressions of her clenched fist raised in anger. The second major financial sponsor was Mark Lane, whose 1966 book *Rush to Judgment*[3] had played a key role in advancing the conspiracy theories

rampant in the years following the JFK assassination. Lane had published a new book, *Conversations with Americans*,[4] featuring interviews with Vietnam veterans who described war crimes and
atrocities. To raise money for the Winter Soldier Investigation, Fonda
and Lane planned a series of fundraising concerts and speaking
appearances throughout the United States prior to the hearings, focusing largely on college campuses.

The VVAW was concerned that journalist Neil Sheehan had just
published a scorching *New York Times Book Review* evaluation of
Lane's book, in which he established without doubt that the book was
full of false tales of war horrors that never happened, based on interviews with supposed veterans who had never seen a day of military
service in Vietnam.[5] Still, the group's only corrective was to require
that "witnesses" provide information about their military units and
where the supposed atrocities had occurred. Witnesses were required
to provide a DD-214 military discharge form as evidence of their military service.

The VVAW picked Detroit to host the Winter Soldier Investigation
precisely because the city had a solid middle-America reputation.
Detroit's gray winter, its smokestacks, and its automobile manufac-
turing plants would serve as a perfect backdrop for what the leftists
wanted to bill as the common man's indictment of the war. Lane had
met with Al Hubbard, an African American veteran who served as
VVAW leader, in the group's headquarters at 156 Fifth Avenue in New
York City. But New York itself was too "Eastern" (meaning, too "liberal") to serve as a stage for the Winter Soldier Investigation. A much
better environment was an everyman's hotel, a Howard Johnson
Motor Hotel, to be precise, located on a middle-class street adjacent
to downtown Motown.

The room chosen for the event had no windows. Concrete support
pillars peppered throughout the room's interior created "restricted

view" spots around which chairs had to be positioned so viewers could observe. On a modest raised platform in front, the "investigators" sat behind a simple wooden table resting on folding metal legs. While the event lacked television media coverage, a radical film crew had set up cameras and lights to shoot a "documentary" intended for later distribution in leftist circles. A few hundred spectators showed up, and reporters from the *Detroit Free Press* were there to cover the event.

John Kerry was at attendance at the Winter Soldiers Investigation. He listened as witness after witness presented incredible horror stories of American soldiers in Vietnam—decapitations; torturing of prisoners; firing artillery on villages for fun; corpsmen killing wounded prisoners; napalm dropped on villages; women raped; innocents, including children, massacred; and tear-gassing people for fun.[6]

Each witness had at least one truly shocking bit of testimony that allowed him to be distinguished from other witnesses, a new level of "Oh my God" horror that was his unique badge of honor. If the tale after tale of unspeakable horror actually happened, then the conclusion was inescapable that the U.S. military had become the natural home for our country's misfits. Why would a psychopath or a sadist do anything but enlist? The opportunity for a target-rich environment for anyone's neurosis was right here, plentifully available to U.S. soldiers serving in Vietnam. The witnesses seemed to recite a certain list of offenses that everyone just knew had happened—village burning, graphic sexual harm to women, the murder of helpless civilians often in unusually cruel manners, torturing prisoners (often in a sexual manner), killing children and babies. Reciting horrors became as an unofficial badge of courage, a required ritual for acceptance into the ranks of the antiwar activists.

The debunking of the Winter Soldier testimony began almost instantly. The *Detroit Free Press* asked for and received from the

VVAW ten days' advance warning on some of the testimony that would be given. The *Free Press*, however, reported as the hearings began that much remained uncertain, that "much of the testimony that will be heard during the three days could not be corroborated by the *Free Press* in the ten days it had to run down each account." And, again, describing the many scattered and isolated stories that the anticipated testimony would present, "Like a soldier jokingly pitching a smoke bomb into a crowd of peasants fighting over a can of discarded C-rations. Or a medic slashing his unit's identification into the flesh of a dead Vietcong soldier. Or the torturing of a prisoner by hooking generator wires to his genitals. Or the rifleman who spread plastic explosives between crackers and handed it out to Vietnamese children as snacks. There are many who may choose not to believe these stories. The Pentagon may refuse or be unable to confirm them primarily because the accounts are so vague that they amount to a 'bucket of steam.'"[7] When the *Free Press* asked, those testifying had presented no affidavits.

At the conclusion of the Winter Soldier Investigation, antiwar senator Mark Hatfield of Oregon was so impressed with the testimony that he insisted the transcript be inserted into the congressional record. Senator Hatfield also called for a military investigation into the charges that had been made. The Naval Criminal Investigative Service (NCIS) conducted the military inquiry. In his 1980 book *America in Vietnam*, Guenter Lewy noted that the NCIS questioned the identities of many of the witnesses who had appeared before the Winter Soldier Investigation. The most damaging finding "consisted of the sworn statements of several veterans, corroborated by witnesses, that they had in fact not attended the hearing in Detroit. One of them had never been to Detroit in his life. He did not know, he stated, who might have used his name." As Lewy concluded, "The VVAW's use of fake witnesses and the failure to cooperate with military authorities and to provide crucial details of the incidents further cast serious doubt on the professed desire to serve the causes of justice and humanity. It is more likely that this inquiry, like others earlier and later, had primarily political motives and goals."[8]

The 1998 book *Stolen Valor: How the Vietnam Generation Was Robbed of Its Heroes and Its History*, by B. G. Burkett and Glenna Whitley, provides a powerful debunking of supposed Vietnam War veterans falsifying or exaggerating their service records and inventing atrocity stories. Burkett served in Vietnam with the 199th Light Infantry Brigade and was awarded the Bronze Star Medal, Vietnamese Honor Medal, and Vietnamese Cross of Gallantry with Palm. He never expected to be an author, nor did he expect to spend ten years researching Vietnam War stories. Still, the many phony stories he was hearing of Vietnam—veterans claiming acts of heroism that never happened, wildly exaggerated war records from supposed soldiers who never served, or, if they did serve, were never in Vietnam—simply stuck in his craw. Burkett characterized the Winter Soldier Investigation as "a classic example of turning reality on its head."[9]

At the Winter Soldier Investigation, more than one hundred "veterans" and some sixteen civilians testified. Burkett reports, for example, that the National Archives can find no service records under the names of eleven of the individuals claiming to be veterans who testified at the Winter Soldier Investigation. This strongly suggests that the eleven were complete frauds, lying that they had Vietnam experience as well as lying about supposed atrocities they witnessed or committed. The likelihood is that these eleven were never in any branch of the United States military at all.

In 1970, joining the VVAW took little more effort than just showing up. Anyone with a beard, a scraggly uniform, and enough make-do information about the military and Vietnam—information readily available in a bar or a library—could become a full-fledged member.

There was no credentials committee and no background search required for membership. If your story was good enough and your demeanor at least reasonably convincing, you might even be permitted to testify in a staged inquiry like the Winter Soldier Investigation. If you were lucky, your story could get into the press, and you would experience a limited form of celebrity, despite the fact that the whole charade was based on a lie.

Both the Winter Soldier Investigation and John Kerry's testimony before the Fulbright Committee played against the national publicity given the My Lai massacre. A military court-martial had just convicted Lieutenant William Calley of murdering twenty-two unarmed civilians in the March 16, 1968, massacre. Rather than seeing this as an isolated incident of extreme violence that was duly punished, the opponents of the Vietnam War preferred to use the incident to support their favorite argument, namely, that all U.S. military personnel in Vietnam were committing atrocities in their normal course of duty.

When Senator Claiborne Pell of the Foreign Relations Committee questioned Kerry about Calley and My Lai, Kerry echoed the theme:

> My feeling, Senator, on Lieutenant Calley is what he did quite obviously was a horrible, horrible, horrible thing and I have no bone with the fact that he was prosecuted. But I think that in this question you have to separate guilt from responsibility, and I think clearly the responsibility for what has happened there lies elsewhere.
>
> I think it lies with the men who designed free-fire zones. I think it lies with the men who encouraged body counts. I think it lies in large part with this country which allows a young child before he reaches the age of fourteen to see 12,500 deaths on

television, which glorifies the John Wayne syndrome, which puts out fighting-man comic books on the stands, which allows us in training to do calisthenics to four counts, on the fourth count of which we stand up and shout "kill" in unison, which has posters in barracks in this country with a crucified Vietnamese, blood on him, and underneath it says "kill the gook," and I think clearly the responsibility for all of this is what has produced this horrible aberration.

Those who were then serving honorably in Vietnam or who had served honorably in Vietnam got John Kerry's message loud and clear: He was painting them all as criminals.

Yet if Kerry's argument was correct and atrocities were the expected direct result of military orders, then Calley should never have been punished; instead, he should have been decorated. After all, Kerry and his VVAW associates were arguing that genocide was a natural consequence of official military policy in Vietnam.

"Gooks" was a derisive term and bears closer scrutiny. A key charge in the antiwar movement's indictment of the Vietnam War was that it was racist. Put in the simplest terms, antiwar activists were charging that America did not value the lives of Asians. As evidence for that argument, antiwar apologists argued that African Americans were disproportionately drafted into the military and put in combat because a racist America sought to wage the war to the disadvantage of our own country's racial minorities.

By 1971, an alliance had formed between antiwar protesters and extremist groups supporting African American civil rights, including the Black Panthers. For a time, the VVAW sought to maintain a middle-of-the-road approach in the protest community, trying to distance itself from the clearly revolutionary and generally Communist groups such as Students for a Democratic Society or the People's Coalition for Peace and Justice. After all, the members of the VVAW were supposedly combat veterans. Still, VVAW members appeared comfortable with their more revolutionary brothers' and sisters' Marxism and Leninism, even if they themselves were not openly Communist.

Kerry and his activist friends also "demonized" American soldiers fighting in Vietnam. As Kerry characterized the situation, the Vietnam veteran returning home was a "misfit," warped by his experiences, doomed to suffer. John Kerry in 1971 was the perfect spokesperson for the VVAW. The American public in 1971 was not ready to listen to yet another fist-clenched, loudmouthed, bearded youth with an angry cause. Kerry was different. He was nicely dressed and well groomed, even when he put on his military fatigues war-protester outfit. That is what was so disarming about John Kerry: One had to listen closely to him to realize he was advocating a very radical position. He invited one to look at him first, to see his mop of thick hair, his lanky frame, his jutting jaw of determination. But there was virtually no substantiation behind his rhetoric.

From virtually nowhere, John Kerry became a star of the antiwar movement. On the day of his Fulbright Committee testimony, the news media was already talking about John Kerry running for president. Kerry had demonstrated that he knew how best to utilize the value of a stage, even if the speech he gave on that stage was nothing but a lie.

Kerry's false allegations had a profound and long-lasting effect on the American public's view of the Vietnam-era military. Soldiers returning from Vietnam were treated with a degree of contempt that has no parallel in American history, and the image of Vietnam veterans as murderous, drug-addled psychotics persists in American culture to this day.

"Skid Row"

Marine First Lieutenant Jim Warner had had a rough time, even for a POW in the gulag of North Vietnam in the spring of 1969. Having been interrogated and tortured for four months by the North Vietnamese, who threatened to hold him after the war for trial as a war criminal, Warner (once the proud backseat navigator of a Phantom jet) had just been transferred by the North Vietnamese to the "place for punishment" outside Hanoi known by the prisoners as "Skid Row." Just as things didn't seem that they could get much worse, they did.

An interrogator confronted Warner with testimony from his own mother and father asking for his return at John Kerry's Winter Soldier Investigation hearings. He told Warner, "Even your parents know you are a war criminal."[10] The interrogator showed Warner a large piece of cardboard with photographs of John Kerry and news clippings relating to Kerry's Senate testimony and demonstrations and said that "everyone knows you are a war criminal." Warner had resisted beyond caring, but he hoped that the North Vietnamese had made it all up. Upon reviewing his mother's testimony in *The New Soldier*, Warner asked: "What kind of ghoul would exploit my mother and family to claim I was a war criminal while I was in a North Vietnamese prison? How could someone do something like this for political advantage?"

Lieutenant General John Flynn, distinguished as one of the three highest-ranking POWs in Vietnam, met John O'Neill at a 1977 party in San Antonio. Lieutenant General Flynn thanked O'Neill profusely for having debated John Kerry in 1971 on the *Dick Cavett Show*, while he had been in captivity in Vietnam. He said that he and his fellow POWs would never forget the lies of Kerry and the VVAW that the North Vietnamese had presented to them to break their spirits. He described the hollow feeling they shared when they saw pictures

or read testimony of their fellow veterans in the United States betray-
ing the bond that sustained them in the POW camps.

Admiral Jeremiah Denton and many other POWs never forgot the
North Vietnamese attempt to use "war crimes" claims from their
own fellow veterans, led by Kerry, against them. Ron Bliss, a POW for
five years, has spent thirty years trying to forget the small cells with
a single speaker and his sense of betrayal and loneliness resulting
from the claims of the North Vietnamese jailers that his military
"comrades" in the VVAW had testified to his alleged guilt. Navy Lieutenant Paul Galanti felt particularly betrayed that a fellow Navy lieutenant would sell him out with false war crimes charges, cited over
and over by the North Vietnamese as proof that he had committed
war crimes and should confess.

Words once spoken cannot be taken back. Kerry's false words, so
conducive to a quick bubble of popularity in 1971, caused untold
grief, beginning first with the POWs languishing in North Vietnamese
jails and then in camps from Laos to Cambodia to the Cau Mau
peninsula of South Vietnam. Many of these POWs never made it
home. John Kerry's words, his book *The New Soldier*, and his organization, the VVAW, likewise gave birth to the now thirty-year-old car-
icature of U.S. soldiers as drug-sated criminals. No foreign enemy
ever dealt so direct and devastating a blow to the morale of America's
armed forces and its veterans than John Kerry did. He struck
directly—and falsely—at the honor of their service, the glue binding
all units together.

Swift Boat Veterans for Truth React

The Swift Boat veterans who came to Washington, D.C., on May 4,
2004, to hold a press conference opposing John Kerry's presidential bid
were strongly opposed, even after some thirty-five years, to Kerry's
antiwar statements:

I served with these guys. I went on missions with them, and these men served honorably. Up and down the chain of command there was no acquiescence to atrocities. It was not condoned, it did not happen, and it was not reported to me verbally or in writing by any of these men including Lieutenant (jg) Kerry.

In 1971–72, for almost eighteen months, he stood before the television audiences and claimed that the five hundred thousand men and women in Vietnam, and in combat, were all villains—there were no heroes. In 2004, one hero from the Vietnam War has appeared, running for president of the United States and commander in chief. It just galls one to think about it.

—Captain George Elliott, USN (retired)

I was in An Thoi from June of '68 to June of '69, covering the whole period that John Kerry was there. I operated in every river, in every canal, and every off-shore patrol area in the 4th Corps area, from Cambodia all the way around to the Bo De River. I never saw, even heard of all these so-called atrocities and things that we were supposed to have done.

This is not true. We're not standing for it. We want to set the record straight.

—William Shumadine

In 1971, when John Kerry spoke out to America, labeling all Vietnam veterans as thugs and murderers, I was shocked and almost brought to my knees because even though I had served at the same time and in the same unit, I had never witnessed or participated in any of the events that the senator had accused us of. I strongly believe that the statements made by the senator were not only false and inaccurate, but extremely harmful to the United States' efforts in Southeast Asia and the rest of the world. Tragically, some veterans, scorned by the antiwar movement and their allies, retreated to a life of despair and suicide. Two of my crew mates were among them. For that there is no forgiveness.

—Richard O'Mara

I served in Vietnam as a boat officer from June of 1968 to July of 1969. My service was three months in Coastal Division 13 out of Cat Lo, and nine months with Coastal Division 11 based in An Thoi. John Kerry was in An Thoi the same time I was. I am here today to express the anger I have harbored for over thirty-three years, about being accused with my fellow shipmates of war atrocities.

All I can say is that when I leave here today, I'm going down to the Wall to tell my two crew members it's not true, and that they and the other forty-nine Swiftees who are on the Wall were then and are still now the best.

—Robert Brant

We look at Vietnam. After all these years, it is still languishing in isolated poverty and helplessness and tyranny. This is John Kerry's legacy. I deeply resent John Kerry's using his Swift Boat experience, and his betrayal of those who fought there, as a stepping-stone to his political ambitions.

—Bernard Wolff

Back to 1971

In the question-and-answer exchange following his prepared statement to the Fulbright Committee, Senator George Aiken of Vermont asked John Kerry what would happen in South Vietnam if America withdrew from the war:

Mr. KERRY:... But I think, having done what we have done to that country, we have an obligation to offer sanctuary to the perhaps 2,000, 3,000 people who might face, and obviously they would, we understand that, might face political assassination or something else. But my feeling is that those 3,000 who may have to leave that country—

Senator AIKEN: I think your 3,000 estimate might be a little low because we had to help 800,000 find sanctuary from North Vietnam after the French lost at Dien Bien Phu.

In 1975, when North Vietnam took over the South, a mass exodus began. Those fearing political repression or fearing for their lives desperately sought to leave the country. An estimated 1.5 to 2 million people set out by sea on anything that would float, risking starvation or drowning. Over a quarter of a million were simply lost at sea. Others were murdered, raped, tortured by pirates. The refugees headed for Thailand, Malaysia, Hong Kong, and the Philippines. As late as 1997, thousands remained in refugee camps scattered across Asia, awaiting naturalization or, even worse, repatriation. If John Kerry and his antiwar associates were correct, if the Vietnamese comprehended no fundamental difference between freedom and Communism, why did so many risk death?

After their victory, the Communists established a network of nearly one hundred "reeducation camps," political prisons in which they incarcerated indefinitely a wide range of former enemies—officials of the South Vietnamese government; bureaucrats and educators; intellectuals, including writers, reporters, and religious leaders; anyone whom the Vietnamese communists considered dangerous because they had supported or worked with the United States to stop the advance of Communism in Indochina. Estimates of the number of people put through these camps range from half a million to nearly one million.

Subsequent to establishing their hold on South Vietnam, the Vietnamese Communists turned their aggressive armies toward Laos, Cambodia, and Thailand, and ethnic minorities were not safe within Vietnam. In the years since 1975, the Vietnamese Communists have waged war on the Montagnards, the Christian mountain people who dared to fight with the United States against Ho Chi Minh.

Yet nowhere in the public record is there any evidence that John Kerry has ever admitted his estimate was wrong—that only three thousand people would have to be relocated to protect them in the event of a communist victory in Vietnam.

Toi Dang, a Vietnamese sailor who served with Kerry and O'Neill in Coastal Division 11 on An Thoi (and in its South Vietnamese successor) from January 1969 until April 1975, remembers the horror of the North Vietnamese takeover. Dang was able to escape to the United States, shorn of his family, heritage, and country. The nineteen people in his unit were all placed in reeducation camps and disappeared forever. His wife's uncle was taken to a camp on the Chinese border where the only allowed tools were bomb fragments. Without food or medicine, almost everyone in the camp soon died. One naval officer from An Thoi was executed for shooing a chicken from his small garden. The Vietnamese sailors of An Thoi—Swift brothers to this day—have a special memory of John Kerry and his testimony. In Dang's words: "His testimony was all lies. He is a brother only to other liars—not to my Swift brothers."[11]

SEVEN

MEETING WITH THE ENEMY

"It is a fact that in the entire Vietnam War we did not lose one major battle. We lost the war at home, and at home John Kerry was the field general."

ROBERT ELDER

Swift Boat Veterans for Truth Press Conference
Washington, D.C., May 4, 2004

I on Mihai Pacepa, the highest-ranking Soviet intelligence officer to defect to the West, spoke out in June 2004 about the KBG intelligence operation that he believed was the basis for the assertions of war crimes and atrocities at the heart of John Kerry's 1971 testimony to the Fulbright Committee.

For Pacepa, the case was clear. John Kerry's 1971 accusations of war crimes in Vietnam sounded to him just "like the disinformation line that the Soviets were sowing worldwide throughout the Vietnam era."[1] The KGB had as a top priority the damage of American credibility in Vietnam. To this end, the KGB spent millions producing "the very same vitriol Kerry repeated to the U.S. Congress almost word for word and planted it in leftist movements throughout Europe."

According to Pacepa, Yuri Andropov, then chairman of the KGB, ordered agent Romesh Chandra, the chairman of the KGB-financed World Peace Organization, to create the Stockholm Conference on Vietnam as a permanent international organization "to aid or to conduct operations to help Americans dodge the draft or defect, to demoralize its army with anti-American propaganda, to conduct protests, demonstrations, and boycotts, and to sanction anyone connected with the war." The Communist Party was funding the World Peace Organization to the tune of about $50 million a year at this time, according to Pacepa, with another $15 million allocated for the Stockholm Conference on Vietnam. In the five years of its existence, the Stockholm Conference "created thousands of 'documentary' materials printed in all the major Western languages describing the 'abominable crimes' committed by American soldiers against civilians in Vietnam, along with counterfeited pictures." The KGB's disinformation department manufactured these materials, and KGB operatives in Europe and America printed up and distributed hundreds of thousands of copies.

Whether Kerry knew it or not, his 1971 testimony to the Fulbright Committee was reciting the Communist Party line chapter and verse. Pacepa left no doubt as to his conclusion: "As far as I'm concerned, the KGB gave birth to the antiwar movement in America."

Vietnam Veterans Against the War

By November 1970, Al Hubbard had emerged as the most prominent national leader of the VVAW. Hubbard professed strong ties to the Black Panthers. Less well known was his involvement with the People's Coalition for Peace and Justice (PCPJ), a militant antiwar organization with decidedly Communist ties. Key among the PCPJ's founders was a group of Trotskyite radicals from the Socialist Workers Party who had first emerged in the 1969 National Mobilization to End the War in Vietnam.

Al Hubbard turned out to be yet another veteran who lied about supposed service in Vietnam. He claimed to be a decorated Air Force captain who had sustained a shrapnel injury in his spine when flying a transport plane into Da Nang in 1966. His story began to unravel when NBC received a tip, and Hubbard had to confess on the *Today Show* that he had really been only a sergeant, not a pilot or a captain, in Vietnam.

At first, John Kerry came to the support of his friend, excusing Hubbard's lie as understandable. Hubbard, Kerry explained, lied because he felt he needed the distinction of rank to be important enough to lead the VVAW. Within a few days, however, the lie completely unraveled. The Department of Defense issued a news release stating that, at the time Hubbard was discharged from the Air Force in October 1966, he was serving as an instructor flight engineer on C-123 aircraft with the 7th Air Transport Squadron, based at McChord Air Force Base in Tacoma, Washington. The Department of Defense reported that: "There is *no record of any service in Vietnam* [emphasis in the original], but since he was an air crew member he could have been in Vietnam for brief periods during cargo loading, unloading operations, or for crew rest purposes. His highest grade held was staff sergeant E-5."[2] Moreover, Hubbard had no Purple Heart or Vietnam Service Ribbon, and the Air Force had no record that he had ever been in Vietnam, although it was possible that Hubbard may have stopped off there on a transport run. As it turned out, Hubbard's injuries were sports injuries—an injury suffered in a basketball game in 1956, and a soccer game in 1961.

John Kerry had appeared side by side with Al Hubbard on NBC's
Meet the Press on April 18, 1971. He had shared the stage with
Hubbard in the VVAW's Dewey Canyon III protest in Washington,
D.C., which had set the stage for his testimony before the Fulbright
Committee. By June 1971, when Hubbard's fraud was becoming
apparent, Kerry was embarrassed, but he continued to represent the
VVAW as its national spokesman, and Hubbard continued to repre-
sent the group as its executive director and national leader.

Kerry in Paris

In June 1971, Lo Duc Tho arrived in Paris to join the North Vietnamese Communist delegation to the peace talks. His arrival marked
a change in the Communists' approach to advancing their goals
through negotiation. Lo Duc Tho was, with Ho Chi Minh, one of the
original founders of the Communist Party of Indochina and one of
North Vietnam's chief strategists.

He arrived to join a comrade, Madame Nguyen Thi Binh, who had
been a member of the Central Committee for the National Front for
the Liberation of the South and was now the foreign minister of the
Provisional Revolutionary Government (PRG) of South Vietnam.
The military arm of the PRG was widely known as the Viet Cong,
and Madame Binh was recognized as the Viet Cong delegate to the
conference.

On July 1, 1971, within days of Lo Duc Tho's arrival, Madame Binh
advanced a new seven-point proposal to end the war. Central to this
plan was a cleverly crafted provision offering to set a date for the
return of U.S. POWs in exchange for the Americans' setting a date for
complete, unilateral military withdrawal from Vietnam. In other
words, America could have its POWs back only if we agreed that we
lost, then surrendered, and then set a date to leave.

About one year earlier, two young Americans had also come to Paris, presumably for their honeymoon: John Kerry, a young, clean-shaven Navy war veteran, accompanied by his new wife, the former Julia Thorne, who could trace her lineage back to George Washington. But honeymooning was not John Kerry's only reason for traveling to Paris. Kerry's presidential campaign has now acknowledged that he "talked privately with a leading Communist representative" there.

For decades, this meeting had been only a rumor. The rumor stemmed from a comment Kerry made in the less publicized question-and-answer segment of his April 22, 1971, testimony before the Fulbright Committee: "I have been to Paris. I have talked with both delegations at the peace talks, that is to say the Democratic Republic of Vietnam and the Provisional Revolutionary Government."

On March 25, 2004, Michael Kranish of the *Boston Globe* reported that Michael Meehan, a spokesman for Kerry's presidential campaign, admitted that John Kerry had traveled to Paris after his May 1970 wedding and, on that trip with his wife, he had a brief meeting with Madame Binh, a meeting that included members of both the Democratic Republic of Vietnam (the North Vietnamese) and the Provisional Revolutionary Government (the Viet Cong). Meehan insisted that Kerry did not go to Paris with the intention of meeting the Communist delegations to the Paris Peace Conference and that he did not involve himself in negotiations. Kerry has insisted that the meeting was solely for "fact-finding" purposes.[3]

On July 22, 1971, Kerry called a press conference in Washington, D.C. Speaking on behalf of the VVAW, Kerry openly urged President Nixon to accept Madame Binh's seven-point plan.[4]

Madame Binh's proposal had been crafted to send a strong emotional message to the American home front—that the only barrier to having our POWs returned was America's own unwillingness to set a date to withdraw, even if the proposed withdrawal amounted to a defeat. The Viet Cong proposal directly challenged the South Vietnamese proposal to set a date for a truce and a free election designed to unite the divided Vietnam. The PRG and the Viet Cong clearly agreed with the premier of Communist China, Cho En-lai, that complete withdrawal of American military forces from Vietnam was the only precondition that would be discussed.

As the *New York Times* noted when reporting on the press conference, John Kerry suggested that President Nixon had refused to set a date for withdrawal because North Vietnam had not guaranteed the return of American POWs. Now that the Vietnamese Communists were promising to set a POW return date, Kerry argued that Nixon had no reasonable course left except to set a date for withdrawing U.S. military forces. Kerry failed to mention one consideration President Nixon most likely found compelling—that America's cause was just and that the interests of freedom might best be served by halting the spread of Communism in Southeast Asia. The United States, in President Nixon's view, had not fought the war to abandon our allies to Communism but to defend South Vietnam's right to self-determination.

Today, presidential candidate John Kerry would have us believe that the only goal of his antiwar activities was to speak up bravely against a war he knew to be without justification. All he wanted to do was to stop a war where military policies such as free-fire zones and tactics such as search-and-destroy led inevitably to war crimes, the killing of innocent civilians, and the burning of peaceful villages. Kerry wants us to believe that he has always been against Communists. Yet the historical record raises questions about both claims.

Loyal Americans think twice about violating the legal provision against negotiating with foreign powers (18 U.S.C. section 953) and the constitutional prohibition against giving support to our nation's enemies during wartime (Article III, Section 3). Anti-Communists do not openly support proposals that amount to an American surrender to Communist enemies, plus a demand to pay war reparations. There is no public record of what Kerry discussed with the Vietnamese Communists in Paris in 1970. Kerry's presidential campaign has refused to provide any detailed account of the discussion, nor has the campaign answered questions regarding who set up the meeting. There must have been contact between Kerry or his representatives and the representatives of the Vietnamese Communists. Which Communists assisted Kerry in arranging his meeting with Madame Binh, and why?

John Kerry may believe in his own mind that his participation in the antiwar cause lifted him to a new moral plane, one where he would not be restricted by conventional legal distinctions or commonsense understandings of patriotism. Yet, the record shows that Kerry and the VVAW consistently coordinated their efforts with Communists, both foreign and domestic, represented the Communist positions, and repeated their grossly exaggerated claims of American atrocities. In fact, it is hard to find any disagreement whatsoever between Kerry's words and actions as a leader of the VVAW and those of the Hanoi and Viet Cong leadership. Had Madame Binh herself been permitted to appear at the July 22, 1971, press conference instead of John Kerry, the most noticeable difference in the argument presented might have been the absence of a Boston accent.

John Kerry was clearly welcomed warmly by the Vietnamese Communists. His propaganda value was obvious—a good-looking, clean-shaven, well-spoken, decorated American war hero. How could any Communist apologist not see that here was the next candidate to carry their anti-American message back home? John Kerry had no difficulty getting an appointment from Madame Binh. The Communists welcomed him.

Coordinating with the Enemy

A major goal of the VVAW in 1971 was sending representatives to Paris or to Hanoi to meet with the enemy.

An FBI confidential surveillance report dated November 11, 1971, was released as part of the twenty-thousand-page file on the VVAW, made available after a Freedom of Information Act request and published on the Internet during the 2004 presidential campaign. This report indicates that the FBI was monitoring Kerry to see if he planned another trip to Paris to meet with the Communist delegations:

> John Kerry and Al Hubbard, members of the Executive Committee, VVAW, were planning to travel to Paris the week of November One Five—Twenty [November 15–20] for talks with North Vietnamese Peace Delegation.[5]

An analysis of the FBI reports made public make clear that the government's concern about the VVAW coordinating their activities with the Vietnamese Communists was founded in facts. The VVAW Steering Committee meeting in Kansas City, Missouri, from Friday, November 12, 1971, through Sunday, November 14, 1971, was a raucous meeting, the dramatics of which are emphasized by recently released FBI undercover investigative files. John Kerry is clearly listed in the FBI reports as one of the five members of the steering committee.

The fireworks started a couple of hours into the meeting, when steering committee member Al Hubbard arrived from the airport by taxicab. Hubbard, one of the VVAW's most controversial leaders, announced to the group that he had just come from Paris, where he had met with the Vietnamese Communist delegations to the Paris peace talks. Hubbard had clearly crossed over to the enemy side. He reported with excitement that he had just concluded negotiations with the Vietnamese Communists, and that they were ready to release a group of American POWs to the VVAW, provided that the VVAW send a delegation to Hanoi around Christmas. Hubbard told the group that the Communist Party of the USA had paid for his trip and that he was now acting as a member of the Coordinating Committee of the People's Coalition for Peace and Justice.

Consider this extract from the FBI files:

Al Hubbard, the reputed original organizer of the VVAW, flew into Kansas City at six thirty PM on Friday, November Twelve, last. He discussed [BLACKED OUT SECURITY EDIT]. His flight, alone, to Paris where he met with Xuan Tui [phonetic], from which trip he had just returned. Xuan Tui, one of the North Vietnamese Delegates to the Paris Peace Talks, and Representatives of the PRG and the DRV spoke to Hubbard. Hubbard said that the PRG represents revolutionaries in South Vietnam and the DRV are North Vietnamese. They wanted to make arrangements for more Americans (presumably VVAW or New Left activists) to travel to North Vietnam. Hubbard also gave the impression that the North Vietnamese would generally support future VVAW actions but gave no other details as to that support.[6]

A follow-up report several days later gave further details:

[BLACKED OUT SECURITY EDIT] advised that Hubbard gave the following information regarding his Paris Trip.

Two foreign groups, which are Democratic Republic of Vietnam (DRV) and Peoples Republic Government (PRG) (phonetic), invited representatives of the VVAW, Communist Party USA (CP USA), and a Left Wing group in Paris, to attend meetings of the above inviting groups in Paris. Hubbard advised he was elected to represent the VVAW. An unknown male was invited to represent the CP USA and an unknown individual was elected to represent the Left Wing group from Paris. He advised at the meeting that his trip was financed by CP USA. Hubbard said while in Paris an individual named [BLACKED OUT SECURITY EDIT] accompanied the visitors and acted as liaison between the visitors and the inviting groups.

Hubbard said while they were in Paris he met with an individual named Swanwee, a representative of North Vietnam. They talked about the POW issue and the possibility that a VVAW delegation might be able to go to Vietnam in the near future and discuss the possibility of the release of American POWs.

[BLACKED OUT SECURITY EDIT] advised that after Hubbard's talk regarding his trip [BLACKED OUT SECURITY EDIT] and John Kerry the [BLACKED OUT SECURITY EDIT][7].

Once again, the "Swanwee" referred to in the report was the phonetic rendition of Xuan Thuy, chief North Vietnamese delegate to the Paris peace talks.

Joe Urgo, a VVAW national staff member, spoke next to the Steering Committee. According to the FBI report, Urgo supported Hubbard's assertion that the Vietnamese Communists were open to VVAW members coming to Hanoi. The FBI report makes it clear that the discussions the VVAW was having with the Vietnamese Communists were aimed at helping the Vietnamese promote the antiwar movement in America. The "Xuan Tui" referred to in the report is most certainly Xuan Thuy, the chief North Vietnamese delegate to the Paris peace talks. The indication is that the VVAW wanted to work with the Vietnamese Communists to advance their goals, not to pursue a separate or different VVAW agenda:

Joe Urgo joined Hubbard in Friday night's discussion and later on Sunday, November Fourteen, Last, Urgo himself said more, regarding the possibility of a VVAW instigated release of Prisoners of War (POW) by the North Vietnamese. It was not specified by either Urgo or Hubbard if such a POW release would be part of the next VVAW trip to North Vietnam, but it is expected that this is the reason for that VVAW trip. Hubbard said that he would know ten days after he left Paris or sometime around November TwentyThree—TwentyFour, next, when in the near future, and how many VVAW members would be allowed to enter North Vietnam, and thus the persons to go on that trip would be designated by VVAW National Leadership at that time. A list of Ten to Twelve was to have been made of persons to prepare for the trip. [BLACKED OUT SECURITY EDIT]

Urgo, who had returned from North Vietnam in August, last, with [BLACKED OUT SECURITY EDIT] of the War Resisters League and [BLACKED OUT SECURITY EDIT] of the Women's Strike for Peace, spoke as if he himself were working for the North Vietnamese officials. Urgo said that the North Vietnamese do not want to shift American New Left emphasis away from the anti-war issue onto any other issue. Thus, they would not want to discuss POW exchange during a VVAW trip to North Vietnam but would rather occupy VVAW visitors with indoctrination.[8]

According to several FBI reports covering these meetings, John Kerry indicates that he was present and heard these discussions. A separate FBI surveillance report, filed on November 24, 1971, provided corroboration of the November 19 report. Again, John Kerry was listed as being present as an executive committee member.

Public records indicate that Kerry continued to represent the VVAW in public speeches through April 1972, nearly five months after learning that Al Hubbard, once one of his antiwar "band of brothers," had crossed over to the Communist side. Nowhere in the FBI files is there any report that the steering committee at the November 1971 meeting ever stopped to discuss 18 U.S.C. section 953, which directly forbids United States citizens from negotiating with foreign powers, or Article III, Section 3, of the United States Constitution, which defines treason in part as giving aid and comfort to the enemy in time of war. It is clear that the VVAW leaders understood the serious nature of their activities. Over the course of the weekend meetings, they relocated twice to avoid surveillance by government authorities. That turned out to be a vain hope, since the FBI had multiple informers inside the meeting.

The FBI surveillance record now made public clearly indicates that the VVAW as of November 1971 was working directly with the enemy against U.S. military objectives in the war. The VVAW did not stop at attempting to undermine support for the war in the U.S. by propagating its false claims of war crimes and atrocities. It was also actively contemplating attempts to effect the release of POWs as further evidence of the correctness of its position and to take steps to actively encourage soldiers in the field to refuse orders to engage the enemy in combat. Producing tapes for broadcast in Vietnam to induce U.S. service personnel to stop fighting indicates both negotiating with the enemy and the intent to give direct aid to the enemy in time of war.

John Kerry, who until recently claimed to have resigned from the VVAW in June 1971, has now acknowledged that he was present, as the FBI reports show and a number of eyewitnesses have claimed. Still, Kerry insists he remembers nothing of the Kansas City meetings, a fault of memory that is remarkable given the nature of what was discussed.

There is also good reason to believe that prior to the Kansas City meeting in November 1971, Kerry himself had made a second trip to Paris to meet with the Vietnamese Communists. Evidence for this comes from Gerald Nicosia, a very pro-VVAW and pro-Kerry historian who wrote a chronicle of the organization called *Home to War: A History of the Vietnam Veterans' Movement.*[9] Nicosia originated the Freedom of Information Act request that led to the FBI making public the twenty thousand–document file on the VVAW and John Kerry. Writing in the *Los Angeles Times* on May 24, 2004, Nicosia noted, "Kerry's public image was perhaps tarnished most in 1971 by his attempts to hasten the return of American POWs. The files record that Kerry made a second trip to Paris that summer to learn how the North Vietnamese might release prisoners."[10]

Discussions of VVAW members traveling to Paris and Hanoi recur throughout the FBI surveillance reports. The discussions make clear that the goal is not just to arrange a release of POWs, but also to enhance the status of the VVAW and to advance the cause of the antiwar movement by the way in which the prisoners would be released to the VVAW. The FBI files now released make one point very clear: John Kerry and his VVAW comrades were welcome guests of the Vietnamese Communists in both Paris and Hanoi, guests who could be counted on to return to America and actively support the leadership of America's wartime enemy.

John Kerry's Antiwar Activities and the Communist Press

The Communist Party of the USA established the *Daily Worker* newspaper in 1924. By the 1970s, the paper was published under a different banner, the *Daily World*. Published in New York, the paper developed stories with a focus on America. Various Communist newspapers around the world republished *Daily World* stories under many different banners. In 1971, the *Daily World* devoted considerable attention to covering John Kerry and the VVAW antiwar activities.

The Communist world understood clearly then what John Kerry even today still tries to deny. The antiwar movement typified by the VVAW was not simply a protest movement. At its core, the VVAW was avowedly anti-American, willing to propagate lies about "war crimes" allegedly committed by American soldiers on a daily basis. The goal that the VVAW was seeking to achieve through its highly publicized demonstrations in Washington, D.C., during April 1971 was to convey one simple message: The United States had lost its moral way in opposing the Viet Cong. Kerry, as spokesperson for the VVAW, was trumpeting the theme the Communist world wanted heard. Navy lieutenant John Kerry could not have been a more perfect poster boy for the Communist *Daily World* than if he had been recruited and trained by the KGB itself.

Today, running for president in 2004, John Kerry can object that the *Communist Daily World* was free to cover whomever it chose, and that he did not seek out the paper's coverage or give interviews to its reporters. Yet, the deeper reality is that anyone literate at the time, anyone deeply involved in the political and moral struggle that was Vietnam, could not ignore the impact of the extensive coverage given by the *Daily World* to the VVAW's Dewey Canyon III April 1971 protest in Washington.

On Friday, April 23, 1971, the *Daily World* ran a front-page photo of John Kerry on the speaker's platform, assisting former U.S. attorney general Ramsey Clark by handing him some papers while Clark addressed a crowd on Capitol Hill. The caption under the photo identified John Kerry as a "former Navy lieutenant and a leader of the group." Ramsey Clark at that time was serving as legal counsel for the VVAW, and the group was actively engaged in a Supreme Court contest trying to prevent an injunction removing them from the

National Mall in front of the Capitol, the spot they had chosen for a campsite during their protest in Washington. The next day, Saturday, April 24, 1971, the *Daily World* ran John Kerry's photograph again on the front page, sitting in a studied pensive pose, his right index finger extended to his cheek, in a serious moment during his appearance before the Fulbright Committee.

Kerry Praises Ho Chi Minh

The FBI field surveillance reports document a speech that Kerry gave in 1971 in which he praised Ho Chi Minh, the founder of Vietnamese Communism. The occasion was a speech Kerry gave to a group at the YMCA in Philadelphia on June 14, 1971. As reported by the FBI:

> On June 29, 1971, [BLACKED OUT SECURITY EDIT] advised that JOHN KERRY of the National Office of the VVAW, spoke at the YMCA, Philadelphia, on June 14, 1971. In this talk he stated that HO CHI MINH is the GEORGE WASHINGTON of Vietnam. Ho studied the United States Constitution and wants to install the same provisions into the Government of Vietnam. KERRY criticized United States activities in Vietnam, saying we are destroying villages, cities, crops, and the people there and these activities must be stopped.[11]

Kerry gave many antiwar speeches in 1971. His tendency to idealize the Vietnamese Communists and to demonize the United States was possibly most apparent when he chose to praise by association with America's founding father the man responsible for introducing Communism to Indochina.

EIGHT

KERRY'S ANTIWAR SECRETS

"Kerry's turncoat performance in 1971 in his grubby shirt and his medal-tossing escapade, coupled with his slanderous lies in the recent book portraying us that served, including all POWs and MIAs, as murderous war criminals, I believe, will have a lasting effect on all military veterans and their families."

CAPTAIN CHARLES PLUMLY, USN (RETIRED)

Swift Boat Veterans for Truth Press Conference
Washington, D.C., May 4, 2004

"My plan was that on the last day at a certain time, probably 11:30 or 2:30 (either right before or after lunch), we would go into the offices—in our schedule with our congressmen, we would schedule the most hard-core hawks for last—and we would shoot them all...I was serious..."

SCOTT CAMIL

VVAW leader and Kerry companion to June, 1971 *Cavett Show* debate; discussing his February, 1971 and November, 1971 formal assassination proposal voted down by VVAW. University of Florida Oral History Program Interview of Scott Camil, Oct. 20, 1992

The VVAW Plot Kerry Doesn't Want You to Know About

At the VVAW steering committee meeting in Kansas City in November 1971, Florida regional coordinator Scott Camil brought up an assassination plan that he had first proposed during the April 1971 Dewey Canyon III event in Washington, D.C. Camil proposed that the VVAW assassinate a group of United States senators who supported the war, including Senator John Tower of Texas, Senator John Stennis of Mississippi, and Senator Strom Thurmond of South Carolina. Camil had termed his plan Operation Phoenix, calling to mind a CIA assassination program in Vietnam that had targeted Viet Cong leadership cadres.

Known as Scott the Assassin, Camil was a firebrand within the VVAW ranks. He advocated the creation of VVAW assassination squads who could emulate the CIA Phoenix Program in Vietnam. The idea, as proposed by Camil, was that the VVAW assassination squads would kill politicians who opposed ending the war, beginning with prominent senators. The problem for John Kerry and the other VVAW members present at the Kansas City meeting was that a conspiracy to commit murder may itself be a crime, whether or not any murder is actually committed. Camil had a well-known fascination with weapons, and his plot may have been more fantasy than reality. Still, those present listened to the proposal and even took a vote on it. Arguably, those present, including Kerry, had an obligation to report the proposed plot to authorities to avoid becoming complicit in a conspiracy to commit murder.

Investigative reporter Tom Lipscomb broke the VVAW assassination story in the *New York Sun* with a series of articles appearing in March 2004.[1] When presented with the details of the assassination plot from the Kansas City meeting, his first reaction was to lie. A spokesperson for the Kerry presidential campaign simply denied that John Kerry had attended the meeting. Then Lipscomb found two VVAW members, Randy Barnes and Terry DuBoise, who had attended the meeting and were willing to go on record stating that they remembered Kerry being there.

Kerry's recent biography, *Tour of Duty*, claimed that he had quit the VVAW on November 10, 1971, several days before the Kansas City assassination meeting, and that his resignation letter was at the VVAW archive in Madison, Wisconsin.[2] The trouble was that nobody could find the November 10 resignation letter in the files. Finally, *Tour of Duty* author Douglas Brinkley admitted to Lipscomb that he did not have a copy of the letter in question; instead, he had been relying on Kerry's own report that the letter existed. To date, no resignation letter has been located. When Lipscomb asked Brinkley who had told him that Kerry was a no-show at the Kansas City meeting, Brinkley's response was that his source was Kerry himself.

At about the time the Kerry presidential campaign was denying that he had attended the Kansas City meeting, the FBI surveillance file on the VVAW and Kerry was beginning to be made available on the Internet. Previously, these records had been available only to Gerald Nicosia, the pro-Kerry writer and VVAW historian who had launched the original Freedom of Information Act request that led to the release of the documents.

As noted in the previous chapter, close inspection of the FBI reports indicates that Kerry was present at the Kansas City meeting as a member of the VVAW executive committee. The FBI reported that Kerry told the steering committee that he planned to resign from the executive committee, but that he would continue to speak for the VVAW and that his resignation from the executive committee would not take effect until a replacement for him had been selected. The FBI file was clear that Kerry was resigning only from the executive committee, not from the VVAW itself.

On Friday, March 19, 2004, writer Scott Canon published an article in the *Kansas City Star* that supported Lipscomb's research. Canon's article suggested that the Kerry campaign was backing away from its initial denial in light of the information in the FBI reports: "A statement Thursday by Kerry's camp said the Massachusetts Democrat did not recall the meeting, although FBI surveillance material and the group's archives clearly show that Kerry resigned from his national coordinator post at that November 1971 meeting."[3] Still, campaign spokesman David Wade tried to save face by advancing a barely believable statement: "John Kerry had no personal recollection of this meeting thirty-three years ago. John Kerry does recall the disagreements with elements of VVAW leadership... that led to his resignation. If there are valid FBI surveillance reports from credible sources that place some of those disagreements in Kansas City, we accept that historical footnote in the account of his work to end the difficult and divisive war."

So, faced with documentary evidence to the contrary, the Kerry campaign quickly shifted ground. The denial that Kerry had attended the meeting was replaced with a convenient statement that he could not recall the meeting—besides, so what, the meeting was a footnote to history. Again the limits of credibility were stretched. This particular footnote to history evidently involved the consideration of a conspiracy to assassinate U. S. senators, something that most people would probably remember for the rest of their lives.

The *Kansas City Star* also reported that John Hurley, an organizer of veteran volunteers for Kerry's presidential campaign, had called several former VVAW members to pressure them to change their stories about the assassination meeting, in particular, one John Musgrave of Baldwin City, Kansas. As the *Star* reported: "I asked him to be very sure of his recollection, not to change his recollection," Hurley said. "I would apologize to John Musgrave if he thought in any way I was pressuring him."[4]

If there was nothing to hide in this Kansas City meeting or in Scott Camil's assassination plot, then why didn't Kerry just tell the truth about the meeting from the start? That Kerry's campaign continues to insist that he has no recollection of the meeting strongly suggests that there is more here that Kerry simply does not want the public to know.

The Medals Kerry Doesn't Want You to Think He Threw Away

The day after John Kerry's testimony to the Fulbright Committee, the VVAW assembled on the front steps of the Capitol for what was to be the culminating event of Dewey Canyon III.[5] One by one, the VVAW protesters approached a microphone and threw their war decorations over a fence into a bin that had been marked "trash." Kerry, too, approached the microphone, said his piece, and threw away a handful of what everybody assumed were his medals.

A film clip of the event in the VVAW short feature *Only The Beginning* captured several of the protesters as they shouted into the microphone before throwing their medals over the fence. The protest was not just political theater; it was angry political theater with a radical antiwar message:

My name's Peter Brannigan, and I've got a Purple Heart here, and I hope I get another one fighting these motherf—ers. (loud cheers)

Robert Jones, New York, and I symbolically return all Vietnam medals and service medals given me by the power structure that has genocidal policies against non-white peoples of the world. (shouts of "Right on!")

22nd Cavalry Squadron in Da Nang, and I hope they realize this is their last G-dammed chance. (cheers)

We don't want to fight any more, but if we do it will be to take these steps! (screams of approval)

The VVAW film clip ends there, to the sound of automatic weapons fire.

Questions about this incident arose when John Kerry ran for the Senate in 1984. Some thirteen years after the medal-tossing demonstration, Kerry found it politically expedient to have his medals back, as evidence of the war-hero status that even in 1984 was at the core of his campaign. Many visitors to Kerry's office reported surprise at seeing Kerry's medals framed and hanging on his Senate office wall. At the demonstration itself, Kerry gave no explanation of what he was throwing over the fence. A reasonable assumption was that he was throwing away his own medals, as were many of the other protesters at the event. No, Kerry explained, he had thrown away only the ribbons he had been wearing on his fatigues; he did not have the medals with him at the time, and there was no time to go home to New York and get them.

Another explanation crept in over the years. Kerry maintained that, yes, he had actually thrown away some medals, but they weren't his own medals; they were the medals of two other veterans he had met. His own medals, he continued to insist, were always in safe-keeping; hence, there was no surprise that they were now on his wall. One more small detail creeps into the story. Sometimes the current location of the medals is described as not on the senator's office wall but in a desk drawer in his study at his home in Boston, or some other office location in Boston, but definitely not lost over a fence.

During the 2004 presidential campaign, the controversy resurfaced when *ABC News* found a 1971 television interview Kerry gave in which he did claim that what he had thrown away during the protest were in fact his own medals. As *ABC News* reported: "I gave back, I can't remember six, seven, eight, nine medals," Kerry said in a November 6, 1971, interview on a Washington, D.C., news program on WRC-TV called *Viewpoints*.

The controversy picked up steam when Kerry appeared on *Good Morning America* and called the whole question a "phony controversy instigated by the Republican Party." He was belligerent, insisting that he was always accurate about what had taken place: "I threw my ribbons. I didn't have any medals. It is very simple." He also said that the military did not make a distinction between medals and ribbons, so he could not understand why the news media was making such a big deal out of it: "We threw away the symbols of what our country gave us for what we had gone through." Now, campaigning as a war hero, Kerry wanted to maintain he had always been proud of his war decorations, even though that was not the impression he gave in the famous 1971 medal-tossing ceremony.[6]

When *ABC News* confronted Kerry with the old videotape from the *Viewpoints* show, he appeared angry. "This is being pushed yesterday by Karen Hughes [former director of communications] in the White House on FOX. It shows up on several different stations at the same time. This comes from a president who can't even show or prove that he showed up for duty in the National Guard. And I'm not going to stand for it," he told ABC's *Good Morning America* while still on the air. When pressed on the discrepancy, Kerry became more combative: "George Bush has yet to explain to America whether or not—and tell the truth about whether he showed up for duty. I'm not going to get attacked on something that I did that is a matter of record." Finally, insisting that he had never said he had given back his combat medals, Kerry insisted, "Back then, ribbons, medals were absolutely interchangeable."

Then, at the end of the interview, when he was off-camera, Kerry made an additional comment that was recorded as he was unclipping the microphone: "God, they're doing the work of the Republican National Committee." Rather than address the contradiction directly, Kerry fell back on what for him was a familiar response technique— he attempted to shift the subject away from himself and the question he had been asked, making the new focus on an enemy presumed to be attacking him.

What is clear is that in 1971, when Kerry was still presenting himself as an antiwar activist, he encouraged the conclusion that he threw his medals away. Ever since he began running for public office, Kerry has wanted those medals back.

Most veterans who win decorations in time of war cherish those decorations as a symbol of the sacrifice they made for their country. Any veteran loyal to America witnessing a demonstration in which veterans threw away their medals would be appalled. After all, this was the purpose of the entire event—to shock America by showing it that Vietnam veterans so little valued their service that they were throwing their decorations in the trash. The April 1971 medal-tossing ceremony in front of the U.S. Capitol was intended as an insult to the American government, a government that the VVAW was directly calling immoral in its pursuit of the war. No one watching the ceremony in 1971 could fail to capture the meaning of the event.

U.S. service personnel were dying that day in 1971 as John Kerry demonstrated in front of the Capitol, and Kerry insulted them by his own act of disrespect. The core of John Kerry's protest in 1971 was what he told the Fulbright Committee: He believed that the war was a mistake. John Kerry wanted the war in Vietnam to end regardless of the outcome. That was his clear meaning, no matter what he threw over that fence. Today, John Kerry wants the American people to see his medals on the wall, as if they had always been there, not his ribbons thrown away in the trash bin.

The New Soldier—
The Book Kerry Doesn't Want You to Read

Late in 1971, MacMillan Publishers brought out Kerry's book *The New Soldier* in a hardcover first edition.[7] John Kerry is listed at the top of the cover page, as author, and the two editors listed are Kerry's longtime friends David Thorne and George Butler. David Thorne, the twin brother of Kerry's first wife, Julia Thorne, first met Kerry when they were freshmen at Yale and are still friends. Thorne continues to advise Kerry in his 2004 presidential campaign. George Butler met Kerry in 1964, introduced through a mutual friend, Dick Pershing. Butler took the photographs in *The New Soldier*, and he has been photographing John Kerry ever since, now over a period of more than thirty-three years.

The New Soldier is divided into several distinct parts. Thorne and Butler wrote the preface. The first major section of the book is an edited version of Kerry's testimony before the Fulbright Committee, testimony that already was in the public domain. The next section of the book presents a chronology of Operation Dewey Canyon III from April 19, 1971, to April 23, 1971.

Dewey Canyon III permitted Kerry to emerge as the national spokesperson for the VVAW, a role that grew out of his visible presence on the stage throughout the event and his televised appearance before the Fulbright Committee on April 22, 1971. Kerry has acknowledged raising approximately $50,000 to cover the expenses of Dewey Canyon III, with the assistance of his friend Adam Walinsky, who had written Kerry's prepared testimony before the Fulbright Committee. Walinsky and Kerry arranged a private meeting with donors at the Seagram Building in New York, a meeting that included Seagram's chief executive, Edgar M. Bronfman Sr., and some twenty New York businessmen who shared Kerry's antipathy to the Vietnam War.

A large section at the core of the book reprints testimony given at the Winter Soldier Investigation, with testimony juxtaposed against photographs of Dewey Canyon III.

The text of the book contains passage after vitriolic passage expressing strong antipathy for the American cause in Vietnam, with charge after charge of war crimes and atrocities, hitting whenever possible the theme that the war was racist in nature. Kerry's epilogue continued the themes of his testimony before the Fulbright Committee:

We will not quickly join those who march on Veterans Day waving small flags, calling to memory those thousands who died for the "greater glory of the United States." We will not accept the rhetoric. We will not readily join the American Legion and the Veterans of Foreign Wars—in fact, we will find it hard to join anything at all and when we do, we will demand relevancy such as other organizations have recently been unable to provide. We will not take solace from the creation of monuments or the naming of parks after a select few of the thousands of dead Americans and Vietnamese. We will not uphold the traditions which decorously memorialize that which was base and grim.

One wonders if John Kerry remembered this passage in 2004 as he attended Memorial Day ceremonies and courted veterans' groups. No wonder suppressing the book has become the order of the day for the Kerry presidential campaign.

A questionnaire appearing at the end of the book is equally radical. Dr. Hamid Mowlana, who administered the questionnaire, admits that only about two hundred surveys were distributed to an estimated 2,300 participants in the Dewey Canyon III demonstration. Only 172 forms were returned, and Dr. Mowlana presents no discussion of any biases he might anticipate regarding which individuals selectively decided to return the questionnaires and which did not, or why this decision was made. No attempt to follow up or conduct additional interviews to correct for bias was discussed. No attempt to sample the Vietnam veteran population in general was made. So we are left with no way to determine whether these protesters were in any way representative of Vietnam veterans as a group.

The respondents are portrayed as young (nearly 75 percent between the ages of twenty-one and twenty-five), educated (nearly 56 percent with some college), Northeastern (54 percent), and single (84 percent). Most were enlisted (65 percent). Most were either students (41 percent) or not working (nearly 37 percent). The key point that the authors drew from the study was that most of the respondents characterized themselves as radical (nearly 49 percent) or extremely radical (an additional 18.5 percent). Over 40 percent reported that their attitudes had begun to change and become more radical during the first three months of their service in Vietnam, 20 percent toward the end of their service in Vietnam, and 16.6 percent upon returning home. In other words, the conclusion was that Vietnam had radicalized the respondents, a conclusion drawn even though Dr. Mowlana and his associate had no way of knowing who actually filled out the questionnaires.

Dr. Mowlana's conclusion, which ends the book, presented as though it were scientifically valid, is that Vietnam was such a terrible experience that those who fought there were overwhelmingly radicalized against the war: "The important thing for this study is the shift of opinion and attitude. In the men, previously characterized as moderates, has developed an attitude by which nearly half of the veterans now accept their position vis-à-vis the political, economic, and social status of the United States as radical. In fact, nearly one-fifth classified themselves as extremely radical."

One of the most incendiary aspects of the book is the photograph on the front of the dust jacket cover, supplemented by a second photo on the inside. Here, we see a ragged group of bearded youths in various types of what appear to be military outfits, carrying an American flag upside down, an international sign of distress, with the demonstrators arranged in a formation that mocks the flag raising at Iwo Jima.

The photograph on the cover was a slap in the face to all those who treasure the legendary photograph taken at Iwo Jima by Joe Rosenthal, as well as to those thousands who every year visit the memorial statue based on his photograph at Arlington Cemetery, dedicated to the memory of all Marines killed in action since 1775. We are drawn to remember that 6,821 Marines gave their lives at Iwo Jima so that these activists, John Kerry included, had the freedom to publish *The New Soldier* with its cover photograph insulting the flag-raising on Mount Suribachi in 1945.

The book's 120 photographs convey the same radical message. In photograph after photograph protesters appear in various makeshift military outfits, holding their clenched fists in the air and shouting in protest. Senator Ted Kennedy appears in one, the only person in a suit, sitting on the ground in a group of ragged protesters, a microphone held forward to capture his words. Al Hubbard and Ramsey

Clark stand on the stage, right hands clasped in what looks like a Black Power salute, with John Kerry standing in the background. We see men and women made up in whiteface, wearing uniforms, carrying what look like toy weapons, moving threateningly as if in hostile fire, presenting what at the time would have been recognized as a street form of guerrilla theater. The photographic messages go hand in hand with the text. Dewey Canyon III gave participating protesters, whoever they truly were, a chance to act out their antiwar, anti-American sentiments in military costume with our nation's Capitol as their stage.

John Kerry first realized what a liability *The New Soldier* could be when he lost his first election, in Lowell, Massachusetts, running for the U.S. Congress against Republican challenger Paul Cronin and a third candidate, Roger Durkin, an independent who dropped out of the race four days before the election and endorsed Cronin. Durkin started the problem for Kerry by running newspaper ads with "CENSORED" stamped over a photograph of *The New Soldier* cover. Durkin wanted to bring to the public's attention that Kerry had refused to grant him the rights to reprint the book's cover in his campaign materials.

Even more than thirty years ago, Kerry and his supporters were prepared to counterattack. Any criticism of Kerry's antiwar activities was considered an "unfair" attack on his patriotism. Yet Kerry himself clearly wanted to keep his radical activism out of the limelight; otherwise, he would have granted Roger Durkin the rights to reprint *The New Soldier* cover, which he had evidently once been proud to put forward. Kerry's defeat in this 1972 congressional race marked the moment when he began to think that running as a war hero might take him farther than running as a war protester. From 1972 on, Kerry attempted to recast his protester days to deny that the triumph of the Communists in Vietnam was ever his goal.

In an op-ed article published in the *Wall Street Journal* on May 4, 2004, John O'Neill wrote:

> John Kennedy's book, *Profiles in Courage*, and Dwight Eisenhower's *Crusade in Europe* inspired generations. Not so John Kerry, who has suppressed his book *The New Soldier*, prohibiting its reprinting. There is a clear reason for this. The book repeats John Kerry's insults to the American military, beginning with its front-cover image of the American flag being carried upside down by a band of bearded renegades in uniform—a clear slap at the brave Marines in their combat gear who raised our flag at Iwo Jima. Allow me the reprint rights to your book, Sen. Kerry, and I will make sure copies of *The New Soldier* are available in bookstores throughout America.[8]

John Kerry's supporters have purchased copies of the book wherever they appear so the book will vanish from circulation. First edition copies typically cost over $1,000 each on Amazon.com and very few are available for sale. On eBay.com, copies of the book have sold for $500 and signed first editions have gone for as high as $1,500. Kerry supporters have gone to extreme lengths to distance him from the book, arguing that it just has his name on it and that he did not actually write it. Yet the book was a collaborative effort between John Kerry and his two good friends of over forty years, David Thorne and George Butler, and Kerry's initials document that he took responsibility for writing the epilogue.

Why has John Kerry sought for so long to suppress his own book, *The New Soldier*? If Kerry were not concerned that his antiwar activism could be a political hindrance, if he did not feel he had crossed the line from responsible protesting to radical activism, then he would have no objection to allowing us the rights to reprint his book. What does John Kerry have to hide?

The War Crimes Kerry Doesn't Want Investigated

The day before the start of the Dewey Canyon III protest on April 18, 1971, Al Hubbard and John Kerry appeared together on NBC's *Meet the Press*. Kerry was directly asked if he himself had committed any war crimes or atrocities in Vietnam. He answered affirmatively that he had. This is the exchange according to the NBC transcript:

MR. CROSBY NOYES (*Washington Evening Star*): Mr. Kerry, you said at one time or another that you think our policies in Vietnam are tantamount to genocide and that the responsibility lies at all chains of command over there. Do you consider that you personally as a Naval officer committed atrocities in Vietnam or crimes punishable by law in this country?

MR. KERRY: There are all kinds of atrocities, and I would have to say that yes, yes, I committed the same kinds of atrocities as thousands of other soldiers have committed in that I took part in shootings in free-fire zones. I conducted harassment and interdiction fire. I used .50-caliber machine guns, which we were granted and ordered to use, which were our only weapon against people. I took part in search-and-destroy missions, in the burning of villages. All of this is contrary to the laws of warfare, all of this is contrary to the Geneva Convention and all of this is ordered as a matter of written established policy by the government of the United States from the top down. And I believe that the men who designed these, the men who designed the free-fire zone, the men who ordered us, the men who signed off on the air raid strike areas, I think these men, by the letter of the law, the same letter of the law that tried Lieutenant Calley, are war criminals.[9]

On May 6, 2004, during the presidential campaign, John Kerry appeared once again on *Meet the Press*. Host Tim Russert replayed for him his April 1971 appearance on the show. The following is their exchange:

MR. RUSSERT: Thirty years later, you stand by that?

SENATOR KERRY: I don't stand by the genocide. I think those were the words of an angry young man. We did not try to do that. But I do stand by the description—I don't even believe there is a purpose served in the word "war criminal." I really don't. But I stand by the rest of what happened over there, Tim.

I mean, you know, we—it was—I mean, we've got to put this war in its proper perspective and time helps us do that. I believe very deeply that it was a noble effort to begin with. I signed up. I volunteered. I wanted to go over there and I wanted to win. It was a noble effort to try to make a country democratic; to try to carry our principles and values to another part of the world. But we misjudged history. We misjudged our own country. We misjudged our strategy. And we fell into a dark place. All of us. And I think that we learned that over time. And I hope the contribution that some of us made as veterans was to come back and help people understand that.[10]

The problem was that in 1971 John Kerry had charged that the Vietnam War was racist in nature, aimed at the Vietnamese people because they were Oriental. That charge had become central to the false image of America fighting an immoral war. Kerry is caught in a dilemma: As a supposed war hero, he would like to repudiate what Kerry the antiwar activist said to the Fulbright Committee and repeated many times elsewhere in 1971 and 1972. Even in trying to distance himself from Kerry the antiwar activist, however, war hero Kerry cannot help from suggesting that war crimes did occur, that the stories told at the Winter Soldier Investigation, despite scholarly debunking, were based in fact. At this point, the argument comes full circle. If the atrocities did occur, and Kerry's comments in 2004 seem to suggest that he stands by his earlier statements to that effect, then Kerry's admission that he personally committed war crimes must remain true as well.

Here the entire argument becomes tortured for Kerry. Even in 1971, when pressed to answer if he had committed war crimes himself, Kerry really had to say that yes, he had committed war crimes himself or at least that he had witnessed them being committed. Otherwise, all his testimony about war crimes was nothing more than hearsay, a recital of what others had said, testimony that he had not verified according to any standards of evidence, legal or academic. The problem was that if Kerry himself had committed war crimes, he might face legal consequences. There is no statute of limitations on murder. If Kerry witnessed war crimes, then he had a responsibility at that time to bring the matter forward to authorities so the offense could be investigated and the responsible parties prosecuted. If Kerry did not come forward in either instance, he was guilty of covering up potentially criminal offenses.

John Kerry has created problems for himself, questions that today he still has not answered. If John Kerry did commit war crimes in Vietnam, what were they? He should come forward with the incidents and accept responsibility for his actions. If he witnessed war crimes in Vietnam, why didn't he come forward at the time? Kerry should list the specifics of what he saw—who, what, when, and where—so the incidents can be investigated as thoroughly as possible thirty-five years after the fact. If John Kerry did not commit war crimes in Vietnam, then why is he lying?

Why Kerry Does Not Want You to Know about His Last Conversation with Al Hubbard

At an impromptu press conference at the Capitol in Washington, D.C., on Thursday, March 11, 2004, Marc Morano, a reporter for CNSnews.com, asked Senator Kerry if he was still in contact with Al Hubbard. Kerry appeared surprised by the question and his response was defensive. He claimed that he had not seen Hubbard since the week of the 1971 *Meet the Press* appearance. Then he defended Hubbard: "To [Al Hubbard's] credit, he did serve his nation. He had simply exaggerated his particular position. But nobody knew it at the time. And those things happen."[11]

As discussed earlier, the Department of Defense finally discredited Hubbard by releasing information that he had been a sergeant, not a captain or a pilot, in the Air Force. Hubbard had not served in Vietnam, and the Defense Department had no record that Hubbard had ever been in Da Nang, let alone received a shrapnel wound landing there. The disclosures about Hubbard were not sufficient to cause the VVAW to throw him out, even after it was revealed that he was not a Vietnam veteran. As has been seen, Hubbard was a major player at the VVAW steering committee meeting in Kansas City in November 1971, where he described to the group the negotiations he had conducted with the Vietnamese Communists in Paris, attempting to effect a release of POWs to the VVAW around Christmas of that year.

Hubbard had become a fixture within the VVAW, even if he was a fraud. Moreover, he was a fraud with Communist connections and strong ties to the PCPJ. According to FBI surveillance reports, at least one of Hubbard's trips to Paris had been paid for by the Communist Party of the USA. Discussion of Hubbard's Communist connections was increasingly appearing in the press. FBI surveillance files record that John Kerry knew about Hubbard's falsifications regarding his service record and his Communist-supported trip to Paris.

Kerry's insistence that he had not talked to Al Hubbard since the week of the Dewey Canyon III protest in Washington, D.C., was not accurate. The FBI surveillance reports clearly indicate that both Hubbard and Kerry were at that historic November 1971 VVAW meeting in Kansas City, and that the two had a heated exchange, prompting Kerry to tell the group that he intended to resign from the VVAW executive committee.

By March 24, 2004, with enough time for investigative reporters and independent researchers to examine the FBI files and to question VVAW members who remembered Kerry and Hubbard being together at the meetings in question, Kerry's presidential campaign spokespersons changed their stories. They now admitted that Kerry had spoken to Hubbard after the week of April 18, 1971, and that Kerry had attended both the St. Louis VVAW meeting in July 1971 and the Kansas City meeting in November 1971 with Hubbard.

Why did Kerry lie when asked when he had seen Hubbard last? Very possibly, Kerry did not want the public to know that he continued to be associated with the VVAW even after Defense Department statements had established beyond doubt that Hubbard was a fraud. If such an important VVAW member had lied about being a Vietnam veteran, then perhaps much of the testimony given at the Winter Soldier Investigation was also a lie. If Kerry left the VVAW over this, would he then have to admit that he had no basis for the statements he had made to the Fulbright Committee that U.S. military war crimes and atrocities were commonplace in Vietnam, a direct result of the chain of command?

Now in the presidential campaign of 2004, Kerry lied (or had a convenient lapse of memory, one sustained for days by his campaign spokesman) and insisted that he had not talked to Hubbard once Dewey Canyon III was over. That was simply not the case.

What John Kerry Does Not Want You to Know about When He Quit the VVAW

The public record indicates that Kerry gave several speeches in 1972 representing the VVAW. The *New York Times* reported on January 12, 1972, that Kerry had given a speech at Dartmouth College, representing himself as a spokesman for the VVAW: "John Kerry, the war critic and spokesman for Vietnam Veterans Against the War, told a Dartmouth College audience of 300 persons here last night to 'get into politics and make the system work.'"[12]

On January 26, 1972, the *Times* reported that Kerry, again representing himself as a spokesperson for the VVAW, participated in a panel discussion organized by Senator Fred Harris of Oklahoma in an event billed as "The People's State of the Union Address." Ralph Nader also participated alongside Kerry as a panelist. The *Times* reported Kerry's antiwar message, continuing to identify him with the VVAW: "John Kerry, a leader of the Vietnam Veterans Against the War, criticized the President for not ending the war at once. 'What was a mistake a year ago or a month ago or a day ago is a mistake now,' he said, 'and one simply does not send men to kill or be killed for a mistake.'"[13]

A full-page advertisement in the *Times* on April 16, 1972, announced an Emergency March for Peace on Saturday, April 22, 1972. The advertisement, paid for by a group named the National Peace

Action Coalition, listed John Kerry as a speaker. An Associated Press report was issued on April 22, 1972, stating, "Antiwar protesters in New York planned a mile-long march from the edge of Central Park to Bryant Park in mid-Manhattan for a rally featuring speeches by John Kerry, a leader of the Vietnam Veterans Against the War and Sen. Mike Gravel, D-Alaska."[14]

By the end of 1971, the VVAW was moving in an increasingly violent direction. A group of sixteen VVAW demonstrators seized the Statue of Liberty in New York on December 26, 1971. Al Hubbard, who even then was still representing himself as the executive secretary of the VVAW, explained the Statue of Liberty takeover to the press: "Through a spokesman at the headquarters, Al Hubbard, a statement was issued that said: 'We, as a new generation of men who have survived Vietnam, are taking this symbolic action at the Statue of Liberty in an effort to show support for any person who refuses to kill.'"[15]

Through the summer of 1972, the VVAW became involved in increasingly radical and violent protests. Consider the following:

• From July 8, 1972, through July 22, 1972, Jane Fonda made her famous visit to Hanoi, where she delivered radio broadcasts to American and South Vietnamese military personnel encouraging mutiny and desertion, while repeatedly claiming that the United States was responsible for war crimes and atrocities. Fonda visited American POWs in Hanoi, reporting in broadcasts from Hanoi that the American prisoners were being "well cared for" and that they wished to convey their "sense of disgust of the war and their shame for what they have been asked to do." A photograph was taken of Fonda sitting in a North Vietnamese antiaircraft gun, wearing a Vietnamese helmet, surrounded by North Vietnamese military. Upon leaving North Vietnam, Fonda accepted from her hosts a ring made from the wreckage of a downed American plane.

- From July 29, 1972, through August 12, 1972, former attorney general Ramsey Clark traveled to Hanoi on behalf of the Stockholm International Commission for Inquiry. Clark denounced the United States bombing of Vietnam and visited American POWs, reporting that their health was good and the conditions of their imprisonment "could not be better."
- In the summer of 1972, both the Democratic and the Republican Parties decided to hold their national conventions in Miami Beach, Florida. The VVAW organized a protest called The Last Patrol, urging VVAW members to travel to the protest campsite set up in Flamingo Park. On the last night of the Republican National Convention, when President Nixon gave his re-nomination acceptance speech, a riot broke out in the streets of Miami Beach, and over nine hundred demonstrators were arrested.

In his campaign for congressional office in Lowell, Massachusetts, John Kerry's early efforts were quite successful. Through winning the Democratic primary for that office in October 1972, Kerry continued to emphasize his antiwar activities and his association with the VVAW. When UPI announced John Kerry's primary victory, he was still being described as a spokesman for the VVAW: "In another race where the Vietnam war was a pivotal issue, John Kerry, spokesman for Vietnam Veterans Against the War, won the Democratic nomination for Congress in Lowell, Mass."[16]

Tom Tiede, a reporter who followed Kerry's campaign in Massachusetts, wrote a UPI article right after Kerry's primary win, when he was strongly ahead in the polls, clearly identifying his association with the VVAW:

Kerry, you'll recall, is the thrice-wounded Vietnam naval veteran (his boat took 188 enemy hits) who brought GIs to the front lines of antiwar battle in 1969. He didn't invent the organization known as Vietnam Veterans Against the War, but he became its most eloquent spokesman. ("I knew the first day I got there it was wrong and I was ashamed to be part of it.") The Kid Korps of America embraced him. So did the national media. He became a new kind of war hero—a man who won a Silver Star for bravery and then gave it back to the government out of resentment for its occasion.[17]

The record shows that up until the time he lost the 1972 congressional contest, Kerry continued to present himself as an antiwar activist. Yet when campaigning for president in 2004, Kerry tried to advance the argument that he had resigned from the VVAW in November 1971. The only reason to advance this lie was to hope that he could disavow VVAW radical activities occurring during the time Kerry associated his name with theirs.

What John Kerry Does Not Want You to Know about His Naval Reserve Status

Early in the 2004 campaign, Kerry presented his Navy service record with a convenient gap. The year 1971 was presented as if John Kerry had no military obligation at this time. The year was important because 1971 was the time of many important VVAW protest activities. Early in 2004, the following language describing Kerry's military service appeared on Kerry's campaign website, www.JohnKerry.com. By June 2004, this paragraph had been removed:

John Kerry is a Decorated Combat Veteran of the Vietnam War: Kerry volunteered for the United States Navy after college and served from 1966 through 1970 rising to the rank of Lieutenant,

Junior Grade. Afterwards, Kerry continued his military service in the United States Naval Reserves from 1972 though 1978.[18]

The year 1971 is left out of the description. This omission was deceptive.

In response to a request by Senator Kerry, the Department of the Navy released a letter detailing the missing period. In a letter dated May 24, 1986, the Navy listed the following:

18 Feb 1966: Enlisted as an OCSA (E-2), USNR (inactive)

19 Aug 1966: Commenced Active Duty as an OCIU2 (E-5)

15 Dec 1966: Honorably Discharged as an OCIU2 to accept commission in United States Naval Reserve

16 Dec 1966: Accepted Commission, Ensign, United States Naval Reserve, continued active duty

16 Jun 1968: Date of Rank as Lieutenant (Junior Grade) (0-2), United States Naval Reserve

1 Jan 1970: Date of Rank as Lieutenant (0-3), United States Naval Reserve

3 Jan 1970: Released from Active Duty, transferred to the Naval Reserve (inactive)

1 Jul 1972: Transferred to the Standby Reserve (inactive)

16 Feb 1978: Honorably Discharged from the United States Naval Reserve as a Lieutenant (0-3)

This record makes it clear that John Kerry was always in the Naval Reserves while he served in the military. He enlisted in the Naval Reserves and was initially inactive. He commenced his active duty in August 1966 and was commissioned as an ensign, again in the U.S. Naval Reserves, in December 1966. John Kerry enlisted in the U.S. Naval Reserves, and he never left the U.S. Naval Reserves.

The letter dated January 2, 1970, releasing John Kerry from active duty and transferring him to inactive duty in the Naval Reserve stated in paragraph six:

> You are advised that your release from active duty does not terminate your status as a member of the U.S. Naval Reserve. On the day following the effective date of your release from active duty as specified in paragraph 3 of this endorsement, you will assume the status of a member of the Naval Reserve on inactive duty. While on inactive duty you are subject to involuntary recall to active duty to the extent authorized by federal statute.[19]

There is an important distinction between being in the Naval Reserves on inactive duty and being in the Standby Reserves on inactive duty. Standby Reserve status would permit a person to argue that he was a civilian for all intents and purposes. A person in the Naval Reserves is still considered in the Navy; inactive duty means that the individual or the unit to which that individual has been assigned has not been called up for active duty. Again, note the similarity: John Kerry, when he entered the Navy on February 18, 1966, entered the Naval Reserves on inactive duty. He did not commence active duty until August 19, 1966.

As a member of the Naval Reserves, Kerry would have held a Naval Reserve identification card; he would have received Navy pay; and he would have had continuing, though minimal, obligations to report to official Navy requests for training and to respond to any

Navy inquiries advanced to him. In 1971, John Kerry was still in the Navy even though his status was Naval Reserves, inactive duty.

To put Kerry's antiwar activities in context, we must remember that he was a member of the Naval Reserves until July 1972, when he was placed on Standby Naval Reserve. Kerry's antiwar activities included:

- Meeting with the enemy in Paris and coordinating ongoing meetings with various members of the VVAW, both in Paris and Hanoi, to arrange the release of American POWs to the VVAW. These meetings also provided aid and support to the North Vietnamese Communists in the form of radio broadcasts and other indoctrination methods aimed at encouraging U.S. soldiers in the field to lay down their arms and desert the military.
- Testifying before the Senate Foreign Relations Committee that the United States was implementing a military policy in Vietnam that caused American soldiers to commit war crimes and atrocities, and that this criminal military policy extended up the entire chain of command.
- Giving a press conference in Washington, D.C., in which he advocated a Vietnamese Communist peace proposal that would have called for a complete withdrawal of the United States military and an abandonment of the government of South Vietnam, in other words, a surrender on enemy terms, followed by the payment of war damage reparations by the United States to the Vietnamese Communists.
- Continuing his representation of the VVAW even after he was aware that various VVAW leaders had falsified their credentials and were not in fact Vietnam veterans.
- Telling many slanderous and otherwise damaging lies in numerous public speeches, the effect of which was to malign the purpose and

morality of the United States service personnel in the field in Vietnam, fighting and dying as he spoke.

- Allowing his speeches and testimony to be used by the enemy in their propaganda efforts, including but not limited to the replaying of these speeches and testimony to American POWs being held in captivity by our enemies.

What is clear from the record is that Kerry lied or otherwise misrepresented his continued service in the Naval Reserves so as to give the impression that he was not affiliated in any way with the U.S. military when he engaged in his radical protest activities. The truth is that Kerry was still in the military when he protested against his own brothers in arms. This raises the additional concern that Kerry's antiwar activities may well have been in direct violation of the obligations of the Uniform Code of Military Justice, which prohibit him from making adverse charges against his chain of command or statements against his country, especially in time of war.

NINE

KERRY'S COMMUNIST HONORS

"I deeply resent John Kerry's using his Swift Boat experience and his betrayal of those who fought there as a stepping-stone to his political ambitions."

BERNARD WOLFF

Swift Boat Veterans for Truth Press Conference
Washington, D.C., May 4, 2004

The Find

War Remnants Museum
Ho Chi Minh City, Vietnam

In the Vietnamese Communist War Remnants Museum (formerly known as the War Crimes Museum) in Ho Chi Minh City, a photograph of John Kerry hangs in a room titled "The World Supports Vietnam in its Resistance." The photograph shows Senator John Kerry being greeted by the general secretary of the Communist Party of Vietnam, Comrade Do Muoi. The story broke over the 2004 Memorial Day weekend. Jeffrey M. Epstein of Vietnam Vets for the Truth acquired the photograph in response to a request for photographs and records detailing Kerry's activities on behalf of the enemy.

Epstein explained the importance of the photograph upon releasing it to the public:

> This photograph's unquestionable significance lies in its place-ment in the American protesters' section of the War Crimes Museum in Saigon. The Vietnamese Communists clearly recog-nize John Kerry's contributions to their victory. This find can be compared to the discovery of a painting of Neville Chamberlain hanging in a place of honor in Hitler's Eagle's Nest in 1945.

Vietnam veteran Bill Lupetti happened upon the Kerry photo when touring the War Remnants Museum in Ho Chi Minh City. Lupetti, who had served as a Navy corpsman working with Swift Boat sailors in An Thoi, was back in Vietnam for the first time since the war, trying to find old friends and visit familiar locations. He took a picture of the Kerry photograph and posted it and a dozen other photographs on an Internet website maintained by Swift Boat veteran Jim Deal. A third Swift Boat veteran, Bob Shirley, copied the photograph from the website and e-mailed it to Jeff Epstein. The research began from there.

The War Remnants Museum was established in 1975. Then called the War Crimes Museum, its principal purpose was to demonstrate what the Vietnamese Communists wanted to represent as American war crimes, including graphic displays of war injuries. Outside the museum is a collection of captured U.S. tanks, airplanes, and heli-copters, as well as bombs and other unexploded munitions. Some of the exhibits are gruesome, in particular one featuring deformed babies that purports to document the effects of Agent Orange laced with thalidomide, a charge advanced by the Communists during and after the war. Even today the museum makes no attempt at balance, even though the name change makes it appear less confrontational, and many of the exhibits are pure propaganda.

Lupetti found the Kerry photograph in a hall dedicated to honoring war heroes who had helped the Vietnamese Communists win in their military struggle against the United States and later against the Chinese. By posting Kerry's photograph in this hall, the Vietnamese Communists acknowledge what they view as his supporting contribution. Across the hall from the Kerry photograph is a photograph of early war protester David Miller, shown burning his draft call-up notice in 1965. The room is filled with banners and antiwar posters from groups around the world whose antiwar demonstrations had helped advance the Communist cause during the Vietnam War.

On the Monday of Memorial Day weekend, May 31, 2004, www.WinterSoldier.com published the Kerry photo on the Internet. The Kerry presidential campaign, as anticipated, declined to comment and quietly questioned whether the photograph had been doctored. Unofficial word from campaign officials suggested that the photograph did not actually appear in the museum. Kerry supporters argued that the photograph really did not demonstrate that the Vietnamese Communists were honoring Kerry for his antiwar protest activity; they contended that the photograph documented Kerry's work for the Clinton administration in seeking to normalize relations with Vietnamese Communists after the war.

We contacted Bill Lupetti in Ho Chi Minh City and asked him to return to the museum to take additional photographs, to document that the Kerry picture was indeed there. We talked with him about the museum and the Kerry photograph:

Q: Bill, is the Kerry photograph still there?

BL: Yes, it sure is. I've been back to the museum four times now, and the Kerry photograph is definitely there.

Q: Does the photograph honor him for his antiwar protests, or for the work he did with Vietnam during the Clinton administration?

BL: Kerry's photo is in a hall of the museum that is called "The World Supports Vietnam in its Resistance." The whole museum is dedicated to the war. There are U.S. tanks and airplanes outside. That particular hall has photos of war protesters like David Miller. There are posters and banners from antiwar groups around the world who supported the Vietnamese Communists in the war. The Communists are saying that everybody in that hall helped them win the war.

Q: What's the photograph next to Kerry's photo?

BL: It's a group of OSS [Office of Strategic Service] guys who in 1945 had trained the Viet Minh to fight the Japanese. They came back to Vietnam in 1995 and had a reunion. It's a propaganda museum; the Vietnamese Communists are saying that these people from around the world supported their resistance movement. The point is that these are the people who helped them win the war and set [up] their Communist government. They're honoring Kerry as being one of the guys who helped them. Kerry is a hero to the Vietnamese Communists. He was a hero to them during the war and he is a hero to them now.

To get independent confirmation, we also contacted Dan Tran of the Vietnam Human Rights Project, who asked associates in Ho Chi Minh City to make sure the photograph of John Kerry was actually in the War Remnants Museum. Tran's contacts confirmed that the photograph is still there.

Tran also asked his Vietnamese associates to get a more precise wording of the placards under the photo. Below are the exact English and French wordings.

Mr. Do Muoi, Secretary General of the Vietnam Communist Party, met with Congressmen and Veterans Delegation in Vietnam (July 15–18, 1993)

Camarade Do Muoi—Secrétaire General du Parti Communiste du Vietnam—recevait une délégation de Sénateurs et Anciens Vétérans du Vietnam le 18 Juillet 1993

We then researched whether Kerry met with Do Muoi any time between July 15, 1993, and July 18, 1993. The Associated Press reported on July 17, 1993, that a U.S. delegation headed by U.S. Deputy Secretary of Veterans Affairs Hershel Gober was sent by President Clinton to Vietnam to deliver microfilm of some three million captured Vietnam War documents that pertained to finding American POWs and MIAs. The article noted that the mission was scheduled to meet with Communist Party general secretary Do Muoi. While the article did not mention Kerry, a White House press release dated July 2, 1993, mentioned Kerry and "a high-level delegation" that included representatives from three major veterans' groups.

In a speech given on the Senate floor on April 29, 1992, Kerry discussed in detail a meeting that he had with Do Muoi in Vietnam to discuss the fate of American POWs and MIAs. A photograph widely circulated on the Internet shows Kerry formally posed with Do Muoi with a statue of Ho Chi Minh in the background.

Thus, the existence of photographs showing Senator Kerry meeting with General Secretary Do Muoi is not in question. In the course of pursuing the POW and MIA issue, it is reasonable that Senator Kerry would seek to meet with the leaders of Communist Vietnam. The critical issue here is that the Vietnamese Communists have chosen to honor Senator Kerry in their War Remnants Museum for his assistance in helping them achieve victory over the United States.

As a senator, John Kerry has consistently supported the Vietnamese Communists, continuing the pattern he established with his antiwar protesting activities. One of the more notable instances of Kerry using his senatorial office to advance the cause of the Vietnamese Communists involves the Vietnam Human Rights Act (H.R. 2833) in 2001. Just days before the September 11, 2001, terrorist attacks on the World Trade Center, the U.S. House of Representatives passed the bill by a vote of 410–1. The bill died in the Senate because John Kerry placed a hold on it and prevented it from coming to the floor for a debate.

In 2003, Representative Ed Royce, Republican of California, reintroduced the Vietnam Human Rights Act, this time as an amendment to a foreign relations appropriation bill, the Foreign Relations Authorization Act (H.R. 1950). In a press release after the bill passed the House, Representative Royce noted what he believed the legislation would accomplish:

Today's vote was a vote of support for all those struggling for human rights and democracy in Vietnam. The stories of persecution and torture at the hands of Vietnam's Communist rulers are staggering and appalling. Innocent people in Vietnam are persecuted because of their religion, ethnicity, or pro-democracy beliefs. This bill is a strike for freedom.[1]

In an effort to promote religious freedom and democracy in Vietnam, the bill will prohibit nonhumanitarian U.S. aid from being provided to Vietnam unless the Vietnamese government begins freeing political prisoners and respecting the rights of ethnic minorities.

The bill also provides additional funding for Radio Free Asia (RFA) to overcome jamming efforts by the Vietnamese government. "RFA will now be better able to bring objective news—the truth—to the Vietnamese people," said Royce.[2]

Once again, John Kerry took active steps to block the bill's passage in the Senate. The Vietnamese Communists have actively fought the legislation every time it has been introduced, arguing that the act constitutes undue meddling in their internal affairs on the basis of fabricated charges. The act's supporters, such as Representative Royce, cite repeated instances in which the Vietnamese Communists have repressed Christians, whom they believe undermine their authority. As Representative Royce has charged, "The stories of persecution and torture at the hands of the Vietnamese Communist rulers are staggering and appalling."

Controversy continues over John Kerry's role in chairing the Senate Select Committee on POW/MIA affairs. In 1993, the commission concluded amid great controversy that there was no "compelling" evidence that any POWs in Vietnam remained alive. As one critic noted:

Through much manipulation and arm-twisting, Kerry persuaded his now-defunct committee to vote unanimously that no POWs existed in Vietnam. And with the disappearance of this and the proposed human rights legislation, Kerry gave Bill Clinton and the Democratic Party the pretext they needed to begin reopening trade that could help keep the Marxist Vietnamese dictatorship afloat. Those given first place in line for such trade opportunities, of course, were the biggest contributors to Democrats such as Senator Kerry and Bill Clinton.

The year after his committee's vote to give Communist Vietnam a clean bill of health, the strangest thing happened. In December 1992, Vietnam signed its first huge commercial deal, worth at least $905 million, to develop a deep-sea commercial port at Vung Tau to accommodate all the trade that was to come. At the time, the chief executive officer of this company was C. Stewart Forbes. Name sound familiar? It should. He is Senator John F. Kerry's cousin. What a coincidence!

Less widely noticed, when the Democratic Party decided to give Kerry a leg up towards its presidential nomination by holding its 2004 National Convention in Boston, certain big corporations rushed to pony up money for the Democratic event. One of the first of these rushing to fill Democratic coffers was Spaulding & Slye Colliers, the current corporate partnership involving Colliers International, which anted up $100,000.[3]

Looking at John Kerry's record in the U.S. Senate since 1984, it is difficult, if not impossible, to find any position he took regarding Vietnam that the Communists would not favor.

Clearly, Kerry's protest activities in the 1970s supported North Vietnam and the Viet Cong in their effort to win the war against America. Today, finding Kerry's photograph in the War Remnants Museum in Ho Chi Minh City is proof of the esteem in which the Vietnamese communists continue to hold Kerry. More than thirty years later, the Vietnamese communists still recognize Senator Kerry's contribution to the continuing success of "their resistance."

TEN

UNFIT FOR COMMAND

"Senator Kerry, we were there. We know the truth. We have been silent long enough. The stakes are too great, not only for America in general but, most importantly, for those who have followed us into service in Iraq and Afghanistan. We call upon you to provide a full, accurate accounting of your conduct in Vietnam."

LETTER TO SENATOR KERRY,
SIGNED BY TWO HUNDRED SWIFT BOAT VETERANS

John Kerry's 1971 testimony to the Fulbright Committee drew immediate criticism from no less an adversary than William F. Buckley Jr. During a commencement address on June 8, 1971, to the United States Military Academy at West Point, Buckley explained to the cadets why he considered Kerry's rhetoric to be simply "the indictment of an ignorant young man" who was willing to level baseless charges that military commanders, three different American presidents, and ultimately the people of the United States had lost their way waging an immoral war in a criminally atrocious manner.[1]

Buckley recognized that Kerry was merely "the crystallization of an assault upon America which has been fostered over the years by an intellectual class given over to self-doubt and self-hatred, driven by a cultural disgust with the uses to which so many people put their freedom." Buckley was certain that the graduating West Point cadets would squarely agree with him that America was worth their sacrifice, and felt that it was essential to repel Kerry's assault, for he saw it as an assault on America itself. "If America is the monster of John Kerry, burn your commissions tomorrow and take others, which will not bind you in the depraved conspiracy you have heard described. If it is otherwise, remember: The freedom John Kerry enjoys, and the freedom I enjoy, are, quite simply, the result of your dedication. Do you wonder that I salute you?"

At the heart of Buckley's argument was that Communism itself was a political system loath to permit the type of freedom that allowed John Kerry to speak so critically. Ronald Reagan was so firm in his opposition to Communism that he dared to call the Soviet Union an "evil empire." Not satisfied to simply contain Communism, Reagan sought to destroy it. Communism, as Reagan saw it, directly opposed the spirit of freedom that breathes in the heart of every human being.

Listening to John Kerry's antiwar rhetoric, we get a distinctly different feeling. Communism is not seen as evil; rather, it is seen as just another political system, possibly somewhat to the left of his own position but nonetheless a legitimate system even if imposed on the people of Vietnam by military force. After all, as he characterized it, the Vietnam War was a civil war in which we were outsiders without the right to choose sides. Michael Lind, a senior fellow at the New American Foundation, expressed the significance of this point: "U.S. public opinion, then, was a key factor both in the disastrous outcome in Vietnam and the successful outcome of the Cold War."[2]

Kerry, as we have seen, urged the United States to surrender and pull out of Vietnam. Basing his charges of atrocities on lies while still a member the Naval Reserves, Kerry broke a fundamental bond of trust with those who remained in the field of combat in Vietnam. Since the days of the Roman Empire, the concept of military loyalty up and down the chain of command has been indispensable. The commander's loyalty to the troops earns him their loyalty in return. How can a man be commander in chief who for over thirty years has slandered his fellow veterans as war criminals? On a practical basis, John Kerry's breach of loyalty is a prescription of disaster for our armed forces.

Today, America is engaged in a new war, a war against the militant Islamic terrorists who attacked us on our own soil. Reasonable people may differ about how best to proceed, but we're sure of one thing: John Kerry is the wrong man to put in charge.

War Crimes: John Kerry's Essential Charge

In every war, war crimes are committed. The key to Kerry's argument during the Vietnam War was that the American military was engaged in systematic war crimes as a direct result of military policies, with approval extending all the way up the chain of command. In other words, Kerry's argument was that policies such as free-fire zones were inherently criminal or that the policies necessarily resulted in combat actions that were criminal. This central point in John Kerry's argument was simply false. Yes, instances of war crimes committed by American military forces in Vietnam have been discovered, and very possibly more will be discovered. Yet when uncovered by the American military, war crimes were investigated, and those involved were punished.

As political scientist Guenter Lewy concluded in his 1978 book, *America in Vietnam*:

The American record in Vietnam with regard to the observance of the law of war is not a succession of war-crimes and does not support charges of a systematic and willful violation of existing agreements for standards of human decency in time of war, as many critics of the American involvement have alleged.

According to Lewy, the charges of systematic war crimes in Vietnam were based on "a distorted picture of the actual battlefield, on ignorance of existing rules of engagement, and on a tendency to construe every mistake of judgment as a wanton breach of the law of war."[3]

We have seen arguments made by Swift Boat veterans who have said rules of engagement for free-fire zones actually placed more demands on responsible commanders in the field and required more fire discipline, not less. A free-fire zone allowed a commander to open fire without being fired upon, but it did not mean that a commander could fire on anything or anyone without exception, without reason, or without justification. Contrary to what Kerry seemed to suggest, a free-fire zone did not compel any soldier to fire.

Kerry's admission that he himself committed war-crimes in Vietnam should be taken very seriously, not as statements intended strictly for political effect, but possibly as honest statements of self-accusation. Still, Kerry carefully qualified every confessional statement by noting that the war-crimes he allegedly committed were the result of the orders he had to obey. In the final analysis, Kerry was not only accusing himself; he was accusing all of us.

Kerry has never dropped the war-crimes theme. Even staffers on his current presidential campaign have fallen into his trap, claiming to have experienced war-crimes even though such claims are most likely baseless. Consider, for instance, John Hurley, who is responsible for organizing veterans to support Kerry's 2004 campaign. Hurley told

Kerry biographer Douglas Brinkley that he too had seen atrocities when with the U.S. Army's 69th Engineers, operating in the Mekong Delta during the Vietnam War.[4]

Tom Pardue, who also served in the 69th Engineer Battalion, challenged Douglas Brinkley on Hurley's assertion. Pardue researched the history of the Army's 69th Engineers and interviewed forty-eight battalion members, and he could find nothing that documented any atrocities or war crimes having been committed or witnessed by the battalion. Pardue wrote to Brinkley, noting that Hurley gave no specific details in his broad accusation that he had seen atrocities. Finally, on May 5, 2004, Pardue sent out a press release noting that Brinkley issued an apology for recording Hurley's statements, and that the publisher, HarperCollins, indicated that the comment would be removed from a revised edition. Pardue was pleased to have gotten a response from Brinkley and the publisher, as Hurley had ignored his repeated telephone calls and e-mails.

Pardue was satisfied with the end result but was still not appreciative of Hurley's comment or how he handled the correction:

Professor Brinkley indicated that Hurley, at John Kerry National Headquarters, faxed instructions to correct the matter. What remains puzzling is that if it was only a simple mistake, why didn't Hurley issue a public correction immediately? Why didn't he talk to us? Now he's claiming that it's Brinkley's error. If so, you would have thought Hurley would have jumped to correct it earlier and not wait months while a group of Vets that served alongside him suffered the undeserved corrosions of their reputations. Thousands of readers were erroneously informed that Hurley saw atrocities in the 69th and Hurley let it drift while the reputation of men who fought, and some who died alongside him were soiled. I know his boss, John Kerry, has been reluctant to discuss retracting claims seeing atrocities. I hope Senator Kerry didn't pressure John Hurley to let a false report that injured the reputations of Vietnam Veterans drift in the wind, in the hopes that the day of retraction would never come.[5]

During the 2004 presidential campaign and during countless earlier campaigns, Kerry has had numerous opportunities to retract his war-crimes claims. Instead, his campaigns continually hunt for any isolated instance anyone can find of a war-crime so Kerry can continue his generalizations about all American troops serving in Vietnam, repeating the same libelous mistake over thirty-five years of unsubstantiated accusations.

Concealment of Records and Current Fraud

A central drumbeat of the Kerry 2004 presidential campaign, as in every Kerry campaign, is that it is relevant and permissible to discuss at infinite length his short Vietnam service and to demand that his opponents discuss their military service or lack of it. Any effort, however, to examine his service by seeking out the records and truth is discouraged and resisted. Kerry has been using precisely the same tactics since 1972.

The reality is that Kerry has consistently refused to disclose his Vietnam records. Instead, he has released only those service records he considers favorable while concealing, for example, his own journal and home movies from the period, except for allowing friendly writers to draw from these materials and providing occasional video clips for advertising.

There is one very simple government form—Standard Form 180— that Kerry could easily execute to permit the Department of Defense to release all his records, such as the many required records for receiving the Purple Heart or Silver Star. By selectively releasing key information and documents, Kerry has tilted the record in his favor. Self-serving journal entries can be presented to "establish" events and circumstances as Kerry wishes to portray them.

A classic Kerry use of his private photographic cache, some of it self-staged, is Kerry's "Lifetime" commercial shown during the 2004 campaign, costing tens of millions of dollars in television time. In this commercial, Kerry is depicted receiving a medal from Admiral Zumwalt (who later denounced Kerry). "Lifetime" also includes a staged clip of Kerry in 1969 as an infantryman in Vietnam, in bandoliers (and violating Rule Number One of the infantry, by pointing his weapon down), stalking an unknown enemy through the forest. Who took this film? When and why? The viewer, typically unskilled in evaluating authentic military images, is left with the impression of Kerry as a fierce warrior engaged in the defense of his country.

Kerry's tactic appears to be designed to provide the media with a prepackaged message of himself as a war hero, a story ready to be spoon-fed to the uncritical or sympathetic voter. Meanwhile, the second prong of the attack takes on Kerry's opponent, whose service record he usually attempts to disparage and belittle.

The Swift Boat Veterans for Truth

On May 4, 2004, a new organization, the Swift Boat Veterans for Truth, held its first press conference in Washington, D.C. About 200 Swift Boat veterans from Kerry's unit signed a petition calling on Kerry to execute Standard Form 180 and allow the public to have complete access to his military service record.[6] The signers of the letter include the entire chain of command above Lieutenant (junior grade) Kerry in Vietnam: Lieutenant Commander Grant Hibbard,

Lieutenant Commander George Elliott, Captain Charles Plumly, Captain Adrian Lonsdale (USCG), and Rear Admiral Roy Hoffmann.

The letter objected to Kerry's activities seeking to criminalize the Vietnam War, including his staged "return" of his military medals. The signers called Kerry's honesty about his conduct in Vietnam into question and challenged his ability to command their respect as commander in chief. Kerry chose to ignore the group. He did not execute Standard Form 180 and he made no personal comment.

Behind the scenes, operatives for the Kerry campaign engaged in personal attacks against the Swift Boat Veterans for Truth and its founders. Wade Sanders, a Swift Boat veteran who has been with Kerry since the days of the Winter Soldier Investigation—a statement by Sanders is included in *The New Soldier*—engaged in an e-mail campaign trying to dissuade Swift Boat veterans from taking part in the May 4 press conference. Salon.com, a website sympathetic to Kerry, published articles claiming that Tex Lezar (a law partner of John O'Neill who had passed away in January 2004) had set up the effort and, with like attention to detail, that Steve Hayes was a Republican operative controlling the Swiftees. Hayes was one of the very few Swiftees who publicly endorsed Kerry in the *Washington Post*. Kerry surrogates explored every conceivable tie to the Republican Party in an attempt to discredit the group as a "front" for the supposed "Republican Attack Machine." Despite protestations by the Swift Boat veterans that no funding or direction had been asked for or received from the Republican National Committee or the Bush-Cheney campaign, the attacks continued.

While the Swift Boat Veterans for Truth press conference was in progress at the National Press Club in Washington, D.C., representatives of the Kerry campaign circulated among the press asking hostile questions, prompting the reporters to use these as the basis of their own questions. The Kerry representatives then invited the press to come immediately afterward to a different floor of the National Press Club, where the Kerry campaign planned to hold its own press conference in response.

Not once in the response to the Swift Boat Veterans for Truth press conference did any representative of the Kerry campaign explain why Kerry had refused to sign Standard Form 180, while the campaign was simultaneously maintaining its attack on President George W. Bush to release his National Guard records.

An Thoi Photograph and Petition

On May 17, 2004, the Swift Boat Veterans for Truth called on Kerry to stop the unauthorized use of their images in national campaign advertising.

For example, a photograph being run in Kerry's television commercials contains twenty officers, including Kerry. Eleven of these men signed the letter condemning Kerry, yet their images were being widely used in Kerry's presidential campaign. The photo was taken on the island of An Thoi on January 22, 1969. These eleven officers, together with Swift Boat Veterans for Truth, called upon Kerry to cease the unauthorized use of the photograph.

Of the remaining eight officers in the photograph, two are deceased, four did not wish to be involved in any manner and one does not support Kerry, but did not have the opportunity to sign the letter above. Only one of the nineteen is believed to support Kerry.

William Shumadine, a member of the Swift Boat Veterans for Truth pictured in the photograph, stated, "John Kerry's use of a photograph with his nineteen comrades, with knowledge that eleven of them condemn him and six who cannot or do not want to be involved, is a complete misrepresentation to the public and a total fraud."

Swift Boat Veterans for Truth displayed three photographs on its website, www.swiftboats.com. The first is the original photograph from An Thoi on January 22, 1969.The second photograph displays each sailor's name over his silhouette and a description of each man's position on the issue. The third photograph shows the one sailor who has agreed to support John Kerry in the 2004 presidential campaign.

Again, the response by the Kerry campaign was to ignore the request to stop using the photograph. Spokespeople for the Kerry campaign contended two points: that the photograph was in the public domain, so Kerry could use it without permission; and second, that the photograph on www.WinterSoldier.com had been altered.

What the Kerry campaign had refused to do was to be honest. Rather than pull the photograph as requested, the Kerry campaign chose to allow the public to have the misleading impression that Kerry was surrounded by Navy buddies who admired him then and now.

Conclusion: Unfit For Command

Many historians have surveyed and rated the record of American presidents as commanders in chief. Filling the shoes of Abraham Lincoln or Franklin Roosevelt when the nation is confronted with a shadowy war on terror is hardly a simple task. It is clear that at the very heart of Lincoln and Roosevelt's success was trust—the simple trust of those dealing with them in their integrity and their genuine concern for those (from the highest to the lowest ranks) serving under them.

The questions about John Kerry extend across several dimensions, but they always end with the problem that, for many veterans, Kerry broke the fundamentals of trust that must be in place to command others successfully.

John Kerry has strangely sought to invoke a heroic Shakespearian image drawn from *Henry V*—a small "band of brothers" outnumbered by a large French army at Agincourt. Imagine how that English army would have felt about a "brother" who had met privately with the French, as Kerry did with the North Vietnamese, while the battle was still joined. Or about a "brother" who left in an abbreviated and controversial way after barely one-third of a normal tour of duty, only to return home and claim that his "brothers" who still remained in combat were war criminals. As the bard wrote in Act IV, Scene III, "He which hath no stomach to this fight, let him depart...we would not die in that man's company."

Why then do we oppose John Kerry in such a public way? It is not so much resentment at his false charges or his exaggerated and fictionalized self-promotion, although this is certainly present. What motivates us is a genuine fear for the consequences to our nation if its safety is placed in the hands of so cynical and shifting a commander in chief.

We were not war criminals, either fighting in Vietnam or remaining here as citizens of the United States during time of war. No man who ever died as an American POW in a North Vietnamese prison was ever forced to hear our testimony in support of the enemy. Yet forgiving and forgetting are not the questions here.

The question is one of fitness and character. The loyalty that is indispensable to successful command cannot simply be restored because a person now wants to be leader. John Kerry might well continue in the Senate, but as commander in chief he has, unfortunately, breached the trust it would take to hold his band of brothers together. In the end, our objection to John Kerry is not his past; it is the future as predicted by his past.

APPENDIX A

**Swift Boat Veterans for Truth
Open Letter to John Kerry**

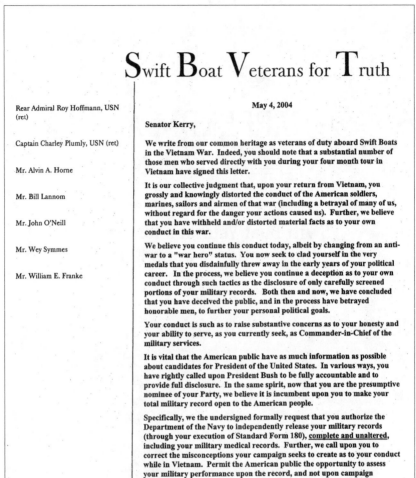

Swift Boat Veterans for Truth

Rear Admiral Roy Hoffmann, USN (ret)

Captain Charley Plumly, USN (ret)

Mr. Alvin A. Horne

Mr. Bill Lannom

Mr. John O'Neill

Mr. Wey Symmes

Mr. William E. Franke

May 4, 2004

Senator Kerry,

We write from our common heritage as veterans of duty aboard Swift Boats in the Vietnam War. Indeed, you should note that a substantial number of those men who served directly with you during your four month tour in Vietnam have signed this letter.

It is our collective judgment that, upon your return from Vietnam, you grossly and knowingly distorted the conduct of the American soldiers, marines, sailors and airmen of that war (including a betrayal of many of us, without regard for the danger your actions caused us). Further, we believe that you have withheld and/or distorted material facts as to your own conduct in this war.

We believe you continue this conduct today, albeit by changing from an anti-war to a "war hero" status. You now seek to clad yourself in the very medals that you disdainfully threw away in the early years of your political career. In the process, we believe you continue a deception as to your own conduct through such tactics as the disclosure of only carefully screened portions of your military records. Both then and now, we have concluded that you have deceived the public, and in the process have betrayed honorable men, to further your personal political goals.

Your conduct is such as to raise substantive concerns as to your honesty and your ability to serve, as you currently seek, as Commander-in-Chief of the military services.

It is vital that the American public have as much information as possible about candidates for President of the United States. In various ways, you have rightly called upon President Bush to be fully accountable and to provide full disclosure. In the same spirit, now that you are the presumptive nominee of your Party, we believe it is incumbent upon you to make your total military record open to the American people.

Specifically, we the undersigned formally request that you authorize the Department of the Navy to independently release your military records (through your execution of Standard Form 180), <u>complete and unaltered</u>, including your military medical records. Further, we call upon you to correct the misconceptions your campaign seeks to create as to your conduct while in Vietnam. Permit the American public the opportunity to assess your military performance upon the record, and not upon campaign rhetoric.

Senator Kerry, we were there. We know the truth. We have been silent long enough. The stakes are too great, not only for America in general but, most importantly, for those who have followed us into service in Iraq and Afghanistan. We call upon you to provide a full, accurate accounting of your conduct in Vietnam.

Respectfully,

Swift Boat Veterans for Truth

Roy Alexander

Kenneth J. Andrews, Lt.

Dan V. Armstrong, BM2

Ray Lewis Ballew

Alexander Bass

George "M." Bates

Richard Beers

Paul L. Bennett, Cdr., USN

Edward J. "Lord Mort" Bergin,
Capt., USNR, Ret.

Henry "Buddy" Berman, QM2

Barry Bogart, EN2

Bob Bolger Cdr., USN, Ret.

M.T. Boone

David Borden

Vern Boyd

David M. Bradley, LCdr.

Robert "Friar Tuck" Brant, Cdr. USN, Ret.

Kenneth Briggs

Carlyle J. Brown , EN2

Kenneth "Buck" Buckholz, GMM3

Michael C. Burton

Joe Cahill, Jr., Lt.

Jack L. Carlson, Lt., USNR

Billy Carwile EN3

Jack Chenoweth

William Colgan, RD3

Bill Collins

Daniel K. Corbett, Lt., USNR

Swift Boat Veterans for Truth

James M. Corrigan, QM3

Terry Cosstello, Capt. USN, Ret.

John H. Davis, Lt.

William K. Daybert, Cdr.

James Deal

John Dooley, Cdr., USN, Ret.

Dale Duffield , BM1, USN, Ret.

Robert G. Elder, Lt.

George M. Elliott, Capt. USNR, Ret.

Wallace Benjamin Foreman, QM1, USN, Ret.

William T. Ferris, Capt. USNR, Ret.

William E. Franke, LT.jg

Robert L. Franson, BMCS (SW)

Alfred J. French, III, Capt., JAGC, USNR, Ret.

Paul F. Fulcomer, RD3

Ray Fuller, GMG3

Steve Fulton, Cdr., USN, Ret.

Mike Gann, Capt., USNR, Ret.

Steve Gardner

Bill Garlow

Les Garrett

Tony Gisclair

Robert Gnau, QM2

Donald Goldberg

Morton Golde, Cdr. USN

Kenneth Golden

Gerald L. Good, Lt. USN

John C. Graves

Charles E. Green, ENCM, USN, Ret.

Swift Boat Veterans for Truth

H.C. Griffin, Jr., Lt. USNR

I.B.S. (Boyd) Groves, Jr.

Charles R. Grutzius, Capt. USNR, Ret.

F.L. Skip "Mustang Sally" Gunther, Lt. USN

Bill Halpin, Lt. USNR, Ret.

Don C. Hammer, Lt.

Rock Harmon

Keith C. Harris, RD2

Stewart M. Harris, Lt. , USN

Gene Hart, RD3

Bob Hastings

Curt Hatler

John Hecker , RD3

Chuck Herman, RD3

Raul Herrera

Tom Herritage

Grant (Skip) Hibbard

Rocky Hildreth

Roy Hoffmann, Adm., USN, Ret.

William P. Holden, Capt., USN, Ret.

Wayland Holloway, Lt. USNR, Ret.

Robert Hooke, Lt.

Andy Horne

John Howell,

Warren Hudson

Charles W. Hunt, EN3

Robert Hunt

Gail E. "Ike" Ikerd, Cdr., Ret.

Warren D. Jenny, RD3

Swift Boat Veterans for Truth

John Paul Jones, QM3

Tom Jones

Eddie Kajioka ENCS USN, Ret.

John L. Kipp, Cdr., USN, Ret.

Thomas H. Klemash

Kenneth Knipple, EN1

Robert Koger, QM2

Mike Kovanen, RD3

Bob Kreyer, GMG2

Jack K. Lane, GMG3

William T. Langham

William Lannom

Joseph R. Lavoie, II CWO2 (BOSN), USN, Ret.

Louis Letson, LCdr., USN, Ret.

Jim Madden, RD3

William S. Mann, Jr., LT.jg

Jim Marohn, GMG3

Douglas Martin, Lt. USNR

Tom Mason, Lt.

Donald Matras, EN2, Ret.

Douglas Martin, Lt. USNR

Thomas Mason, Lt.

Louis Masterson

Richard McFarland, Lt. USNR

Kenneth B. McGhee

James McNeal, ENC

Larry Meyer

Jack Merkley, Lt.

James M. Miller

Swift Boat Veterans for Truth

Martin Miller, ENC, Ret.

Marc Milligan, GMG2

Benjamin A. Montoya, QM3

Bub Morgan, Lt.jg

Edgar (Ed) M. Morrill, Jr.

Tom Morrill, EN3

Kurt Moss, Lt. J.G.

Frank Mueller

Marc Mulligan, GMG2

Ed Mundy

Richard Olsen, Lt.

John O'Neill

Albert Owens

Tedd Peck, Capt. USNR, Ret.

Robert Phalen, GMG2

Joseph L. Ponder, GMG-2, USN, Ret.

Charles Plumley

Chuck Rabel

Bill Rogers , Lt.

Jennings Rogerson II, Capt. USMC, Ret.

Patrick Sage GMG3

Gary W. Sallee, BM2

Joe Sandoval, GMG3

Jimmy W. Sanford, RD3

Robert "Bob" Sattergood

Jim Schneider, EN2

Clair J. (Pete) Schrodt, Capt. USN, Ret.

Jack Shamley

Patrick Sheedy, Cdr., USN, Ret.

Swift Boat Veterans for Truth

Paul Shepherd, QM2

Robert B. Shirley, Lt.jg

William Shumadine

Stanley G. Simonson, GMG2

Darryl Skuce, GMG2

John J. Skura

Gerald H. Smith

Roy Smith

B. Tony Snesko BM2

Mike Solhaug

Jack Spratt, LCDR

H.R. Stirlin, BM2

Fred E. Stith, USN, Ret.

David R. Stefferud, Capt., USN, Ret.

James Steffes

Lawrence Stoneberg, Lt. USN, Ret.

Weymouth Symmes

W.P. (Sonny) Taylor

James P. Thomas

Eldon Thompson, Lt.jg

Charles R. Tinstman, ENC

Gary E. Townsend

Michael Turley, BM2

Chris J. Vedborg, RD3

Jeffrey M. Wainscott, Lt. J.G.

David Wallace

Greg Ward, EN2

Larry J. "Waz" Wasikowski,
Cdr. U.S. Naval Reserve

Pete Webster

Swift Boat Veterans for Truth

Robert T. Wedge, Jr., QM1, USN, Ret.

Pete Webster

George H. White, II

R. Shelton White, Lt.

Gary K. Whittington, EN3

James D. Wiggins

Dennis D. Willess, EN3

Thomas A. Withey, Lt.

Barnard Wolff

Thomas W. Wright , Cdr., USN, Ret.

John Yeoman, Lt.

Ex Officio:

Verne DeWitt

David P. Marion , CPT Infantry, US Army

Benjamin A. Montoya, QM3

Cordelia Ogrinz, in memory of her brother
Alexander J. Ogrinz, III, Lt.

Rex Rectanus, VADM, USN, Ret.

Skip Ridley

Emmett Tidd

James M. Zumwalt in memory of Elmo Zumwalt,
Sr. and Elmo Zumwalt, Jr, his father and
grandfather

APPENDIX B

**Chronology:
Kerry's Naval Career and Involvement
with Vietnam Veterans Against the War**

1966

February 18, 1966: Kerry enlists in the U.S. Naval Reserves, status "inactive" after request for deferment is denied

Spring 1966: Kerry delivers antiwar oration at Yale

August 19, 1966: Reports to officer candidate school in Newport, Rhode Island

December 16, 1966: Commissioned Ensign, status "active"

1967–1968

June 1967–June 1968: Claimed "One-Year Tour of Vietnam" served on the U.S.S. *Gridley*

* June 1967–November 1967: *Gridley* operates on the California coast

* November 1967 –December 1967: *Gridley* sails to the Pacific and operates off the coast of Vietnam (about 5 weeks)

* January 2, 1968 –June 8, 1968: *Gridley* sails to Australia and returns to Long Beach, California

November 17, 1968: Ordered to Coastal Squadron One, Coastal Division 14, Cam Ranh Bay, South Vietnam

December 2, 1968: Purple Heart Medal #1 "combat incident" at Cam Ranh Bay.

December 6, 1968: Ordered to An Thoi on Phu Quo Island, location of Coastal Division 11, Kerry becomes officer in charge of PCF 44

December 13, 1968: Ordered to Cat Lo (north shore of Cape Vung Tau) at Cam Ranh Bay, location of Coastal Division 13.

December 24-25, 1968: Christmas "not" in Cambodia. Kerry at Sa Dec, more than 50 miles from Cambodia

Searched for Bob Hope USO in Dong Tam base

1969

Early January 1969: Kerry reassigned to An Thoi

January 19-20, 1969: Sampan incident where father and child were killed, Cua Lon River in An Xuyen Province

Early February 1969: Assigned commander of PCF 94

February 20, 1969: Purple Heart Medal #2 incident at Dam Doi Canal

February 28, 1969: Silver Star received in incident at An Xuyen Province on PCF 94 (with PCF 23)

March 13, 1969: Purple Heart #3 and Bronze Star Medals incident during Sealords operation with Coastal Division 11, on PCF 94 with four other PCFs in Bay Hap River in An Xuyen Province; "pulled" Rassmann out of water.

March 17, 1969: At Kerry's own request, departs An Thoi for the United States citing three Purple Heart regulation

Fall 1969: Requests early departure from the U.S. Naval Reserves in order to run for Congress

1970

January 3, 1970: Status changes from "active" duty to "inactive" duty in the Naval Reserves

Spring 1970: Runs for Congress but withdraws

First meeting with North Vietnam officials in Paris

1971-1972

March 1971: VVAW meeting where first assassination proposal is made (proposal voted down)

April 19-23, 1971: Operation Dewey Canyon III protest in Washington, D.C., where Kerry throws away his medals or ribbons

April 22, 1971: Testifies before Senate Foreign Relations Committee

June 30, 1971: Debates John O'Neill on *The Dick Cavett Show*

Fall 1971: Begins second run for Congress

November 12-14, 1971: Attends VVAW meeting where a formal proposal is made to assassinate U.S. senators (proposal voted down)

Late 1971: *The New Soldier* is published

July 1, 1972: Transferred to Standby Reserve, "inactive"

NOTES

CHAPTER ONE: DEBATING KERRY

1. Douglas Brinkley, *Tour of Duty: John Kerry and the Vietnam War* (New York: William Morrow, 2004), 370–73.
2. Ibid., 403.
3. Michael Kranish, Brian C. Mooney, Nina J. Easton, *John F. Kerry: The Complete Biography by the Boston Globe Reporters Who Know Him Best* (New York: Public Affairs, 2004), 136.
4. In the debate, Kerry invented a number of lies out of whole cloth, such as a purported mutiny at CosDiv 11. (See Kranish, 92). He gave an impassioned speech about the two-week deliberative process he followed after his third "wound" in deciding whether to allow the Navy to move him after he was told that he could return. In reality, Kerry requested reassignment out of Vietnam on March 17, 1969—as soon as he could get back to An Thoi after March 13 (when he faked his third Purple Heart) and get the form prepared. (See Brinkley, 461).
5. I have been kidded unrelentingly by both friends and family over the white socks and light-colored suit I wore at the debate. It was not a fashion choice. Unlike the well-tailored Kerry, I had only one suit and, therefore, an easy choice. I have noted to my family that David Letterman also often wears white socks on his television show.

CHAPTER TWO: THE RELUCTANT WARRIOR

1. Samuel Z. Goldhaber, "John Kerry: A Navy Dove Runs for Congress," *Harvard Crimson*, February 18, 1970.
2. Douglas Brinkley, *Tour of Duty: John Kerry and the Vietnam War* (New York: William Morrow 2004), 65.

3. J. F. Kelly, Jr. "Living with His Anti-war Past. Should John Kerry become commander-in-chief?" *California Republic*, June 20, 2004.

4. Michael Kranish, Brian C. Mooney, Nina J. Easton, *John F. Kerry: The Complete Biography by the Boston Globe Reporters Who Know Him Best* (New York: Public Affairs, 2004), 77.

5. Authors' interview with Commander Grant Hibbard, June 17, 2004.

6. Brinkley, 158.

7. Although the Associated Press has filed suit to compel the release of Bush's National Guard records, it will not carry stories on Kerry's refusal to execute Standard Form 180.

CHAPTER THREE: THE PURPLE HEART HUNTER

1. E-mail from John Howland, April 20, 2004.

2. E-mail from Van Odell, Gunner PCF 93 and 10, CosDiv 11, May 11, 2004.

3. E-mail to Admiral Hoffmann from Gary Townsend, April 27, 2004.

4. http://www.johnkerry.com/communities/veterans/service.html.

5. Douglas Brinkley, *Tour of Duty: John Kerry and the Vietnam War* (New York: William Morrow, 2004), 147.

6. Ibid.

7. Ibid., 147–48. Ellipsis in original.

8. Ibid., 148.

9. Michael Kranish, Brian C. Mooney, Nina J. Easton, *John F. Kerry: The Complete Biography by the Boston Globe Reporters Who Know Him Best* (New York: Public Affairs, 2004), 71.

10. Ibid., 75.

11. Ibid., 72–73.

12. Ibid., 74.

13. Kerry's campaign has tried to deny Dr. Letson's treatment of Kerry by pointing to the different signature on Kerry's medical report. The report was signed by the corpsman assigned to Dr. Letson, Jess Carreon, now deceased, according to U.S. Navy records.

14. Telephone interview with Grant Hibbard, June 17, 2004.

15. Statement of Louis Letson, M.D., former Lt. Cmdr. [Medical Corps] U.S. Naval Reserve, April 30, 2004.

16. Brinkley, 152.

17. Ibid., 153.

18. Ibid., 185.

19. Statement of William Franke, March 29, 2004.
20. John Kerry, floor speech to the U.S. Senate, March 27, 1986.
21. John Kerry, writing in the *Boston Herald*, October 14, 1979.
22. Kranish, 84.
23. Brinkley, 213–18.
24. After December 16, 1968, there are no other entries of action or signifi-
    cant occurrences involving PCF 44 in the CTF 115 Quarterly Report.
    This, of course, once again indicates the total fabrication by Kerry of
    his mission to Cambodia.

CHAPTER FOUR: WAR CRIMES

1. Douglas Brinkley, *Tour of Duty: John Kerry and the Vietnam War* (New
   York: William Morrow, 2004), 166.
2. Ibid., 269.
3. Ibid.
4. Ibid., 269–70.
5. Brinkley, 202.
6. Michael Kranish, Brian C. Mooney, Nina J. Easton, *John F. Kerry: The
   Complete Biography by the Boston Globe Reporters Who Know Him
   Best* (New York: Public Affairs, 2004), 90–91.
7. It is simply speculation as to why Kerry did not pick up the sampan or
   appear earlier. In Brinkley, 229, Kerry relates a practice of sleeping until his
   boat was on patrol.
8. Michael Kranish, Brian C. Mooney, Nina J. Easton, *John F. Kerry: The
   Complete Biography by the Boston Globe Reporters Who Know Him
   Best* (New York: Public Affairs, 2004), 91.
9. E-mail from Jack Chenoweth, April 21, 2004.
10. Statement by William Franke, March 19, 2004.
11. Statement by Thomas W. Wright, April 16, 2004.
12. Ibid.
13. Brinkley, 259–60.
14. Written statement by Roy Hoffmann, June 19, 2004,
15. Kranish, 92.
16. Ibid.
17. Brinkley, 298.
18. Brinkley, 178.

CHAPTER FIVE: MORE FRAUDULENT MEDALS

1. Telephone interview with Steve Gardner, June 19, 2004.
2. Douglas Brinkley, *Tour of Duty: John Kerry and the Vietnam War* (New York: William Morrow, 2004), 230.
3. Ibid., 205.
4. Ibid., 287.
5. Michael Kranish, Brian C. Mooney, Nina J. Easton, *John F. Kerry: The Complete Biography by the Boston Globe Reporters Who Know Him Best* (New York: Public Affairs, 2004),95.
6. Samuel Z. Goldhaber, "John Kerry: A Navy Dove Runs for Congress," *Harvard Crimson*, February 18, 1970.
7. Silver Star Citation, quoted in Brinkley, 294–95.
8. In Kranish, Fred Short, a Kerry crewman, indicated that the Viet Cong was still armed with an RPG. Many Swiftees claimed that Short said, "Now the VC did not point the B-40 at us...He stood up shocked and booked it...How he ran with some several M-60 rounds in the back of his legs had to be pure adrenaline. His legs looked like hamburger." Short later denied this account, which Dave Wallace and other Swiftees swear they received from him by e-mail in 2002, shortly before he met with John Kerry. Since the young wounded Viet Cong killed by Kerry was the only Viet Cong observed in front of PCF 94 and had just fired a rocket at PCF 94, it obviously would have been difficult to instantaneously reload. Kerry has claimed that he somehow brought the rocket back to the United States as a souvenir. The accounts provided to ABC *Nightline* by Kerry's crew are close to the 2002 e-mail, except the crew speculates that the fleeing, wounded Viet Cong teenager might have turned and fired—possible, but unlikely. They also indicate that the boat would have blown up—completely untrue.
9. Statement of other crewmen to ABC *Nightline*, June 24, 2004.
10. Indeed, it is a little difficult to understand the mental gymnastics involved when Kerry today condemns them as GOP operatives for signing the May 4, 2004, Swift Boat Veterans for Truth letter), when in 1996 Kerry solicited the same men who then were defending him against war crimes charges in 1996. Admiral Zumwalt, who died in 1998, was represented by Lieutenant Colonel James Zumwalt, USMC, his sole surviving son, who signed the May 4, 2004, letter on his father's behalf. During his life, Admiral Zumwalt made his low opinion of Kerry clear to many, including John O'Neill.
11. Virtually all documentation required for a Silver Star in 1969 is missing—either withheld by the Kerry campaign or nonexistent. This documentation includes the nomination form for a Silver Star, the required

official investigation, or the required statements of two witnesses.
Given Kerry's refusal to execute Standard Form 180 to permit direct
release of these records, it is uncertain whether these records are simply being withheld or are nonexistent. It is certain, however, that the
normal documentation accompanying such an award has never been
released.

12. Reporter Charles Sennott claims to have viewed a re-enactment of the
incident, staged by John Kerry with the 8 mm home movie camera he
took with him to Vietnam. This 8 mm home movie re-enactment has
yet to be featured in a 2004 Kerry presidential campaign commercial,
contrasted with the home movie of Kerry walking in Vietnam dressed
as an infantryman, M-16 in hand. The actual after-action report on the
February 28, 1969 incident, like the report on the January 20, 1969 junk
massacre, is among the missing records not found on the Kerry 2004
presidential campaign website, reflecting once again Kerry's selective
release of his service records.

13. Kranish, 105.

14. Brinkley, 313.

15. Statement of William Franke, Swift boat veteran, CosDiv 11, Silver
Star recipient.

16. The repeated statements that Kerry was "sent home" by the Navy
ignore the fact that Kerry requested to be sent home, invoking a regulation of which most Swiftees were unaware.

17. Brinkley, *Tour*, p. 329.

18. John Kerry on the *Dick Cavett Show*, June 30, 1971 [emphasis added]

19. See Kerry website, www.JohnKerry.com, under Service Record, request
for early release dated November 21, 1969. "I've been offered an opportunity to become a candidate for Congress."

20. Until recently, the Kerry presidential campaign website
www.JohnKerry.com had listed the January 29, 1969 battle as Kerry's
battle, despite the fact that Kerry was not there. Michael Kranish of the
Boston Globe pointed out the error, and subsequently the Kerry website corrected the error.

CHAPTER SIX: A TESTIMONY OF LIES

1. J. F. Ter Horst, North American Newspaper Alliance, "A Tale of 2 Veterans: One has Charisma, One Sleeps on the Ground," *Omaha World
Herald*, Thursday, May 6, 1971. A photocopy of the article was found
by researcher Max Friedman in the VVAW files of the House Internal
Security Committee, a document from Files and References materials,

Record Group 233, Records of the House of Representatives, Boxes 750-752, Organization Files/VVAW.

2. John M. Glionna, *Times* Staff Writer, "Vietnam War Illuminates, Shadows Kerry's Campaign. Long after the divisive war, veterans take sides over the Democrat's duty and dissidence," *Los Angeles Times*, February 17, 1971.

3. Mark Lane, *Rush to Judgment*, New York: Holt, Rinehart & Winston, 1966.

4. Mark Lane, *Conversations with Americans*, New York: Simon & Schuster, 1970.

5. Neil Sheehan, Review, "Conversations with Americans," the *New York Times* Book Review, Dec. 27, 1970.

6. Testimony of Scott Camil, *The Winter Soldier Investigation: An Inquiry into American War Crimes*, Beacon Press, 1972, p. 12. As we will see, Scott Camil was a radical members of the VVAW who later proposed to assassinate United States Senators.

7. William Schmidt, "Vietnam Atrocity Hearings Begin in Detroit," *Detroit Free Press*, Jan. 31, 1971.

8. Guenther Lewy, *America in Vietnam*, New York: Oxford University Press, 1978, p. 317.

9. B. G. Burkett and Glenna Whitley. *Stolen Valor: How the Vietnamese Generation was Robbed of its Heroes and its History*. Dallas, Texas: Verity Press, Inc., 1998, p. 113.

10. The "testimony" of Mrs. Virginia Warner is printed in *Vietnam Veterans Against the War, The Winter Soldier Investigation: An Inquiry into American War Crimes*, Beacon Press, 1972, pp. 135-36. Mrs. Warner is quoted as saying:
    "What would you and I do, if a Vietnamese plane flew over and bombed our town? How would we react to somebody that we've captured?" Mrs. Warner's "testimony" was also reprinted in John Kerry's book, *The New Soldier*, New York: The Macmillan Company, 1971, p. 110. This is the testimony the North Vietnamese used to confront Marine First Lieutenant Jim Warner as they tortured him in the Hanoi prison known as "Skid Row."

11. Statement of Toi Dang, July 6, 2004

CHAPTER SEVEN: MEETING WITH THE ENEMY

1. Ion Mihai Pacepa, "Kerry's Soviet Rhetoric: The Vietnam-era antiwar movement got its spin from the Kremlin," The National Review Online, NationalReview.com, February 26, 2004.

2. Burkett and Whitley, *Stolen Valor*, pp. 136-37.

3. Michael Kranish and Patrick Healy, "Kerry Spoke of Meeting Negotiators in Paris," *The Boston Globe*, March 25, 2004.
4. "Anti-War Veteran Accused of Exploiting P.O.W. Issue," *New York Times*, July 23, 1971.
5. FBI Confidential Surveillance Report, November 11, 1971
6. FBI Surveillance Report, November 19, 1971
7. FBI Surveillance Report, November 24, 1971
8. FBI Surveillance Report, November 19, 1971
9. Gerald Nicosia, *Home to War: A History of the Vietnam Veterans' Movement*; New York: Crown Publishers, 2001.
10. Gerald Nicosia, "Veteran in Conflict," *Los Angeles Times*, May 23, 2004.
11. FBI Surveillance Report, June 7, 1971

CHAPTER EIGHT: KERRY'S ANTIWAR SECRETS

1. Thomas H. Lipscomb, "How Kerry Quit Veterans Group Amid Dark Plot," *New York Sun*, March 12, 2004, p. 1.
2. Douglas Brinkley, *Tour of Duty*, p. 406.
3. Scott Canon, "Kerry Hedges on 1971 KC Meeting," *The Kansas City Star*, March 19, 2004.
4. Ibid.
5. The VVAW chose a military name to suggest that they, supposedly veterans, were not attacking the government of the United States. An explanation is given in John Kerry's book, *The New Soldier*: "Operation Dewey Canyon I took place during January and February 1969. During a five-day period in February, elements of the Third Marine Division invaded Laos. Operation Dewey Canyon II was the name given to the first seven days of the South Vietnamese invasion of Laos in February 1971. The name of the operation was subsequently changed. Operation Dewey Canyon III took place in Washington, D.C., April 19 through 23, 1971. It was called 'a limited incursion into the country of Congress.'" John Kerry, *The New Soldier*, "Chronology: Operation Dewey Canyon III" page 26.
6. Brian Ross and Chris Vlasto, "Discarded Decorations: Videotape Contradicts John Kerry's Own Statements Over Vietnam Medals," ABC-NEWS.com, April 26, 2004.
7. *John Kerry and the Vietnam Veterans Against The War*, edited by David Thorne and George Butler, *The New Soldier*, New York: The MacMillan Company, 1971. Hardcover. First Edition Copyright: Vietnam Veterans Against The War, Inc. Library of Congress catalog number 76-171990.

8. John O'Neill, "Unfit For Office," *Wall Street Journal*, May 4, 2004.
9. John Kerry, *Meet the Press*, April 18, 1971.
10. John Kerry, *Meet the Press*, May 6, 2004.
11. Quoted in "Questions for Kerry," an Editorial, The *New York Sun*, March 16, 2004, p. 8.
12. "War Critic, at Dartmouth, Bids Audience Join Politics," The *New York Times*, January 12, 1972, p. 26.
13. Warren Weaver Jr., "A Dozen Dissidents Criticize the President and the Government in 'the People' . . .," *New York Times*, January 26, 1972, p. 17.
14. Richard Boudreau, Associated Press Writer, "Demonstrators to Move Protest to the Streets," *Edwardsville Intelligencer*, Edwardsville, Illinois, Saturday, April 22, 1972.
15. Robert D. McFadden, "War Foes Seize Statue of Liberty," *New York Times*, December 27, 1971, 1.
16. United Press International, widely published, September 20, 1972.
17. "John F. Kerry . . . The Candidate Who's Got It All Going," by Tom Tiede. UPI report, with a dateline Lowell, Massachusetts, widely published on October 25, 1972.
18. www.johnkerry.com [language now removed from the site]
19. Letter of 2 January 1970, U.S. Navy, signed by T. Vanstrydonck, archived on JohnKerry.com.

CHAPTER NINE: KERRY'S COMMUNIST HONORS

1. Press Release from U.S. Representative Ed Royce, dated June 16, 2003
2. Press Release from U.S. Representative Ed Royce, dated June 16, 2003
3. Lowell Ponte, FrontPageMagazine.com, January 28, 2004

CHAPTER TEN: UNFIT FOR COMMAND

1. William F. Buckley, Jr., "John Kerry's America," a Commencement Address to the United States Military Academy at West Point, June 8, 1971. The speech is printed in: *Let Us Talk of Many Things: The Collected Speeches*.
2. Michael Lind, Vietnam: *The Necessary War*, New York: Simon & Schuster, 1999, p. 107.
3. Guenther Lewy, *America in Vietnam*, New York: Oxford University Press, 1978, p. 268.
4. *Tour*, p. 439
5. Tom Pardue, Press Release, May 6, 2004.
6. Letter to Senator Kerry, signed by about 200 Swift Boat Veterans, Swift Boat Veterans For Truth, May 4, 2004

ACKNOWLEDGMENTS

M any people have contributed to this book. We particularly appreciate Admiral Roy Hoffmann and more than sixty Swift boat veterans who spent countless hours providing their recollection of the events involved. We recognize that, for many, this was a painful exercise. Scott Swett, editor and manager of WinterSoldier.com, has been very generous in sharing the extensive research that he has posted on the website concerning John Kerry's involvement in the antiwar movement during the 1970s. Max Friedman, a member of the Historians of American Communism, a group of professional historians, provided invaluable insight into the origins of the American antiwar protest movement in the 1970s. Also important to our locating key research documents was Ed Schamel of the Center for Legislative Analysis at the National Archives in Washington, D.C. Claudia Standiford provided expert editorial assistance as we assembled the manuscript. We, as so many others, are indebted to the insight of Marji Ross who saw the possibilities of turning our work into a book. Harry Crocker, Rowena Itchon, Paula Decker, Amanda Larsen, alongside many other professionals at Regnery, applied their skill and talents to refining our words into published form, doing so within record time.

INDEX